Beauty
and the bike

First published 2009 by
Darlington Media Group
Darlington Media Workshop
DarlingtonArts Centre
Vane Terrace
Darlington, Co. Durham
DL3 7AX
dmg@mediaworkshop.org.uk
www.mediaworkshop.org.uk

This hardback edition published 2009

ISBN 978-0-9564327-0-4

Printed and bound in Germany by Margreff Druck und Medien, www.margreff-druck.de

climateneutral
www.climatepartner.com

Beauty
and the bike

Beatrix Wupperman & Richard Grassick

My Personal Bicycle Journey

Kid's Paradise: The Bicycle Shop

The smell of chain oil and wheel rubber, the faint tinkling of tools, a woman in a blue boiler suit and men with oily hands. That was my childhood dream world, my bicycle shop at the corner. This was where I bought my first scooter at the age of four, after protracted negotiations with my mother. She wanted my long hair cut short. So I made a deal – a scooter for my pony tail. From then on, I visited this shop daily, and dreamt of getting my own bicycle. But the family couldn't afford it, so when I was five I inherited my mother's old bike, a black "retro"-bike, the kind that today is the dream of so many young women. It was far too big for such a small child. To be able to use it, my elder brother took off the saddle and fixed a child's saddle to the vertical bar, 20 centimetres beneath the normal height. No stabilizers and no sparkly bits, but it was my bicycle!

Mein Weg zurück zum Fahrrad

Kinderparadies Fahrradladen

Der Geruch von Kettenöl und Reifengummi, die leisen, klirrenden Geräusche der Werkzeuge, eine Frau im Blaumann und Männer mit leicht verölten Händen, das war meine Kindertraumwelt, mein Fahrradladen an der Ecke. Meinen ersten Roller hatte ich hier mit vier erstanden, mir ertrotzt, denn nur unter der Bedingung war ich bereit, zum Frisör zu gehen, um mir die Haare kurz schneiden zu lassen, für den Roller tauschte ich meinen Pferdeschwanz in einen Pagenkopf ein. Und danach ging ich immer wieder in diesen Laden, erträumte mir mein Fahrrad, die nächste Stufe nach dem Roller. Doch ein neues Fahrrad war unerschwinglich, und so erbte ich mit fünf Jahren das alte Rad meiner Mutter. Es war völlig überdimensioniert für so ein kleines Kind, und damit ich das Rad überhaupt benutzen konnte, wurde mir ein Kindersattel 20 Zentimeter tiefer an die Sattelstange geschraubt.

Suddenly lifted half a metre up, my heart thumping, and moving forwards at the same time, I learned to cycle very fast. So I wobbled up and down our street to the rhythm of my pedals, each wobble just averting the approaching collapse of the whole crazy procedure. But my perspective on this world was suddenly elevated, as though I had suddenly grown up.

Then when I was nine years old, on Christmas 1961, I finally got my "own" bike. The following Easter, I went to secondary school. But it was further away than my primary school. Quite logically, I wanted to use my new red bike to get to school. And so my bike became my main means of transport.

The Zeitgeist was not in Favour of the Bicycle

But this was the 1960's. The car was the future. Not only were we witnessing an enormous building programme of motorways and trunk roads throughout Europe, but also a striking reduction in public transport facilities. All over Europe, from Edinburgh to West Berlin, tram and local rail systems were being ripped up. At the same time cities and towns were being reshaped to make it easier to use the car. This was the age of the urban motorway, slicing whole communities out of existence or out of connection with the rest of their town. The leading idea was "predict and provide". The prediction was a huge growth of cars on the roads, the provision was more, bigger, and wider roads.

Keine Stützräder, keine „sparkly bits", kein Klimbim an diesem Rad, aber es war mein Fahrrad! Ich lernte das Fahren schnell, wenn auch mit klopfendem Herzen, denn plötzlich stand ich einen halben Meter höher und bewegte mich auch noch vorwärts, ich wackelte die Straße entlang, auf und ab im Rhythmus der Pedale, immer in der Gefahr zu straucheln, aber meine Perspektive auf diese Welt war mit einem Schlag erhöht, ich war mobil und glücklich, wenn auch unter gefährlichen Umständen.

Das erste wirklich nutzbare Fahrrad bekam ich dann mit neun Jahren, Weihnachten 1961, und von da an hatte ich immer ein Rad. Mit knapp 10, Ostern 1962, kam ich aufs Gymnasium, das lag weiter weg als meine Grundschule, und ich erkämpfte mir das Recht, mit meinem Fahrrad zur Schule fahren zu dürfen. In meiner Kindheit bin ich sehr viel Fahrrad gefahren, es war mein Haupttransportmittel.

Der Zeitgeist war dem Fahrrad nicht wohl gesonnen

Die Zahl der tödlichen Autounfälle war in den 60er und 70er Jahren auf ihrem Höhepunkt, und trotzdem war der Zeitgeist dem Auto sehr zugetan und überhaupt nicht fahrradfreundlich, galt doch das Auto damals in ganz Europa als das modernste Fortbewegungsmittel. Wir erlebten in dieser Zeit nicht nur einen massiven Ausbau der Autobahnen und anderer Fernstraßen sondern auf der anderen Seite einen ebenso gravierenden Rückbau des Öffentlichen Personennahverkehrs.

Fast überall in Europa wurden Straßenbahnen stillgelegt, ihre Schienen zugeschüttet. Gleichzeitig erleichterten alle Städte das Autofahren, die Straßen wurden breiter, und ganze Stadtviertel fielen der Abrissbirne zum Opfer, um vierspurige Durchgangsstraßen mitten durch die Städte zu legen. „Predict and Provide" war das Motto, es wurde ein enormes Wachstum des motorisierten Individualverkehrs (MIV) vorausgesagt und die entsprechenden Straßen hierfür zur Verfügung gestellt. Dieser Ausbau der Infrastruktur für Autos war fatal, denn heute wissen wir, dass Straßen Autos anziehen, den motorisierten Verkehr verstärken. Das Ergebnis ist Stau statt Erleichterung. Die Politik der 60er und 70er Jahre hat überall in Europa mit ihren Verkehrsprognosen und dem vorauseilenden Straßenbau das Problem geschaffen, mit dem wir heute zu kämpfen haben.

Natürlich gab es vereinzelt erfolgreichen Widerstand gegen die Kahlschlagpolitik in den Städten: In Bremen haben Anfang der 70er Jahre mutige BürgerInnen die „Mozarttrasse", eine geplante Hochstraße mitten durch ein Wohnquartier verhindert, die Hochstraße durch die Innenstadt wurde trotzdem gebaut, sie ist eines dieser oben beschriebenen Altlasten einer autogerechten Stadtplanung.

Die Opfer dieser Politik waren FußgängerInnen und RadfahrerInnen, ihre Infrastruktur wurde vernachlässigt, ihre Spiel- und Bewegungsräume brutal eingeschränkt. Auf der Straße, in der ich geboren wurde, konnte ich als Kind noch Rollschuh fahren, das ist heute völlig unmöglich, alle Fußwege und die Straße sind zugeparkt, und es herrscht nahezu Durchgangsverkehr: Kein Rollschuh berührt

Opposition to these developments was localised and sporadic.[11] Communities fighting against the destruction of their homes, environmental groups against the destruction of natural habitats, could not compete with the wider love affair with the car. The tram and the bicycle were supposed to go the way of the horse and cart.

Then an interesting thing happened. Transport experts, asked to draw up new "predict and provide" scenarios for the 21st century, forecast exponential growth, requiring impossibly expensive new roads. They discovered that more road space simply attracted more cars, accelerating the growth in motorised traffic. The result was not relief, but more congestion. Towns and cities in particular, simply didn't have the space. Even the most car-loving politicians in Europe, Margaret Thatcher amongst them, had to listen to their advisers.

For the average European citizen, on the other hand, these policy battles were, and still remain, well off the radar. In many ways the car's dominance has crept up on us all. There was no great debate about who had priority in our streets when I was young. In the street where I was born, I could roller skate in the middle of the road as a child. Today that is impossible. Today, its pavements, and the street, are filled with parked and moving cars. It has degenerated into a through road, a rat run for cars. My home street is virtually privatised, exclusively reserved for one user group: cars.

On the other hand, countries like the Netherlands, and some cities and towns in Denmark and Western Germany, worked against the 1970s and 1980s trend. Amsterdam and Groningen in the Netherlands, Copenhagen and Odense in Denmark, Münster and Bremen in Germany, all demonstrated what could be done. The material world shapes our ideas, they said; id est, a well built cycling infrastructure gets people out of their cars and on their bikes, just as all the roads have tempted them to use cars in the first place. "Give space on and beside roads to the bicycle, make cycling as attractive as possible and make it more difficult for car drivers to get from A to B", was the motto of this new transport policy. Predict and provide began to be applied to bicycle traffic, as a means of solving the raft of social, spatial, health and environmental problems generated by the car. The hope was that people would change their minds, get out of their cars and onto their bicycles.

---

1 E.g. in Bremen a strong local group fought in the 70s successfully against a flyover right through a residential area: the "Mozarttrasse" would have killed it. Today it is a very wanted central quarter: "Das Viertel".

heute noch diese Straße. Die Straße ist kein öffentlicher Raum mehr, sie ist quasi privatisiert, nur einer Nutzergruppe, den Autos exklusiv vorbehalten.

Ein wenig Heilung für die Zerstörung öffentlichen Raumes brachten die Fußgängerzonen für die FußgängerInnen, das Fahrrad hatte jedoch in fast ganz Europa das Nachsehen. Natürlich gab es Ausnahmen, Länder wie die Niederlande und Städte in Dänemark und Deutschland steuerten in den 70er und 80er Jahren gegen diesen Trend. Die These der Verkehrspolitik auf diesen Inseln der Vernunft war und ist, dass das Sein das Bewusstsein schafft, dass eine gut ausgebaute Fahrrad-Infrastruktur die Menschen aufs Fahrrad bringt, so wie die Straßen sie in die Autos gelockt hatten. „Gib dem Fahrrad Platz auf und neben den Straßen, mach das Radfahren so attraktiv wie möglich, und mach es schwerer, mit dem Auto überall hin zu kommen", das war das Motto einer neuen Verkehrspolitik. Das Thema „predict and provide" wurde hier auch auf den Fahrradverkehr angewendet mit der Hoffnung auf den Sinneswandel der AutofahrerInnen.

Zurück aufs Fahrrad in Bremen

Diese Erfahrungen, diesen Sinneswandel habe ich persönlich „durchgemacht", als ich nach meiner Universitätszeit von West-Berlin nach Bremen zog. Berlin war in den 70er und 80er Jahren keine fahrradfreundliche Stadt, ich selbst fuhr nur in meiner Freizeit durch die Berliner Forsten und an den Seen entlang Fahrrad. Den Weg zur Universität, wo ich studierte und später arbeitete, legte ich meist mit dem Auto zurück. Es gab nicht sehr viele Radwege und keine entwickelte Fahrradkultur,

My Way Back to the Bicycle in Bremen

Personally I went through this change of mind when I moved from Berlin to Bremen. 1980s West Berlin was not especially bicycle-friendly. Yes, I cycled for leisure through the forests and alongside the lakes at weekends. But for my trips to university, where I studied and later worked as a researcher, I used a car. There were few cycle paths and no cycling culture, not even amongst students. Then in 1988 I moved to Bremen, where I encountered a world I'd never seen before: cycle paths all over the city, considerate car drivers, and cyclists everywhere of every age, gender and social class. Then there was the problem of finding a parking space for my car in my residential area. Coming home from work, I would rarely find a space for it anywhere near my house. It seemed there was little point in keeping a car any more, and the alternatives were actually more convenient. So I sold my car, and joined the Stadtauto Car Club for the rare occasions I needed access to a car or van. The fact that cycling was both normal and easy for everyone and anyone, made it a natural part of my everyday life. If a road was busy, there was inevitably a cycle path alongside it. Cars used smaller residential streets, but driving habits were geared to cyclists and children also using them. In fact, many young children passed my flat on their little bicycles on their way to school.

Living near the river, what also struck me was the vibrant teenage life out on the river banks. Hundreds of young people gathered there whenever the weather permitted. Most of them cycled there. The bicycle was clearly a tool of emancipation and liberation, giving teenagers genuine freedom and independence from their parents. Girls grabbed this opportunity just as much as boys.

auch nicht unter StudentInnen.

Mit 36 Jahren kam ich nach Bremen, und dort erlebte ich eine Fahrradwelt wie ich sie bisher nicht kannte: Überall Radwege, rücksichtsvolle AutofahrerInnen und FahrradfahrerInnen aller Altersstufen, beiden Geschlechts und aus allen gesellschaftlichen Schichten. Die Stadt Bremen hat heute 650 km Radwege – das sind doppelt so viele Kilometer Radwege wie in dem heute als „cyclernes by" (Fahrradstadt) vielgepriesenen Kopenhagen – und dazu eine erkleckliche Anzahl von Radrouten im Grünen. Ich fuhr von nun an nur noch Fahrrad.

Darüber hinaus konnte ich mein Auto in meinem Stadtviertel nur unter Mühen parken, und ich vermied, es überhaupt zu bewegen, weil ich beim Nachhause kommen oft keinen Parkplatz fand. Das Auto verlor im Grunde seinen Sinn, die Alternativen Bus, Straßenbahn und Fahrrad waren hervorragend, und so verkaufte ich mein Auto und trat dem Verein „Stadtauto" bei, einer Car Sharing Organisation. Sie heißt heute Cambio und hat mittlerweile rund 5000 Mitglieder in Bremen, rechnerisch teilen sich mehr als 40 NutzerInnen ein Auto von Cambio. Vorsichtig geschätzt ersetzt ein Car Sharing Auto bis zu zehn PKW.

Why British Girls Stop Cycling

Reality Shock in Darlington/England

Marriage in 1998 introduced two country-living to me. My husband, needing to stay in Darlington in Northeast-England, and I myself staying in Bremen, meant continually switching between the two. Naturally I took my bicycle with me because I wanted to use it there as I do in Bremen.

Darlington is a town with 100,000 inhabitants. It offers excellent geographical conditions for everyday cycling. It is relatively flat, less than 7 kilometres across, with relatively mild winters. From this perspective, there is no reason why the inhabitants of Darlington should not be happy everyday cyclists.

But reality was very different. There was no infrastructure for cyclists; if I wanted to get from A to B as quickly as possible, I had to mix with cars on busy roads. But car drivers seemed not to be

Warum Mädchen in Großbritannien aufhören Fahrrad zu fahren

Realitätsschock in Darlington/England

Als mein Mann 1999 nach Darlington in Großbritannien zog, wohnte ich von da an auch zeitweilig in dieser nordenglischen Stadt. Ich nahm mein Fahrrad mit - in der Absicht, es dort genauso zu nutzen wie in Bremen. Darlington, eine Stadt mit rund 100.000 EinwohnerInnen, bietet ideale Voraussetzungen fürs Fahrradfahren: Sie verfügt über eine flache Topografie, und kein Weg innerhalb der Stadt ist länger als 7 Kilometer, mit dem Fahrrad sind das vielleicht 20 bis 25 Minuten von einem Ende der Stadt zum anderen bei gemütlichem Tempo. Natürlich regnet es in England, aber das kommt auch kaum häufiger vor als in Bremen oder Holland. Die Winter sind auf der britischen Insel eher mild, Schnee und Frost sowie eisige Straßen gibt es ganz selten. Von diesen

prepared for a cyclist's appearance on "their" roads. I regularly found myself in very dangerous situations. So I started to cycle on pavements, only to be confronted with angry pedestrians. Repeatedly I explained that the road was too dangerous for me and there were no cycle paths. They did not understand. But I did not give up and eventually helped found Darlington Cycling Campaign in 2004. Today this campaign has more than 100 members and is a respected voice in the town.

Like most towns in the UK, cycling as a means of everyday transport, declined in Darlington to a low of 1% in 2003. Tellingly, the decision by the local authority to try to reverse this trend was taken for environmental reasons, rather than because of the failure of predict and provide. In 2004, the town was named as one of three "Sustainable Travel Demonstration Towns". Then Cycling England chose it to be one of six "Cycling Demonstration Towns". Together this meant more than £6 extra million for sustainable transport modes (public transport, walking and cycling), with the key stress on cycling. Since October 2005 Darlington has been spending £10 per year per inhabitant just for cycling.[2]

This is an excellent basis to improve conditions for cyclists, reduce car traffic and hence help the community to better quality of life. Of course, it is widely recognised that 50 years of pro-car policies cannot be undone in 4 years. In fact, much of the work that has been done in Darlington since 2005 has been data collection. Darlington's data work, organised by the local authority's transport officers with the data firm Socialdata, has been of national importance. [3] The results of Darlington's first 4 years of Sustainable Travel work are positive. The share of local journeys taken by car has fallen by an impressive 6%, walking has increased by 4%. And cycling has nearly tripled from 1% to 3%, but it is still on a very low level. [4]

British Girls Rarely Cycle

Cycling in Darlington is still dominated by men. Two percent of women cycle, whilst men use a bike for five percent of their trips.[5] National statistics explain this trend very clearly. Boys and girls use bikes as toys when they are children, but tend to give it up as they become young adults. But the drop in use amongst teenagers is almost total amongst girls. On average, girls between 11 and 16 cycle 13 times a year, boys 46 times. Between the age of 17 and 20 the figure falls to just 5 trips per year for girls and 29 for boys.[6] Like many towns and cities, Darlington has implemented

2   See Local Motion (Ed.): Cycling Town Review 2005/2009, page

3   Darlington has excellent data material about the travel behaviour of its inhabitants at its disposal: See Socialdata/Sustrans: Darlington - Sustainable Travel Demonstration Town. Travel Behaviour Research. Baseline Survey 2004. Report for Darlington Borough Council, February 2005 and Socialdata/Sustrans: Darlington – Sustainable Travel Demonstration Town. Travel Behaviour Research. Final evaluation report for Darlington Borough Council, March 2009

4   See Socialdata: Darlington 2009, p. 19

5   See Socialdata: Darlington 2009, Table 15

6   See Department for Transport (Ed.): National Statistics. Cycling. Personal Fact Travelsheet – January 2007

Merkmalen her gesehen gibt es keinen Grund, warum die EinwohnerInnen Darlingtons nicht begeisterte FahrradfahrerInnen sein sollten.

Der Realitätsschock war dann aber groß: Es gab keinerlei Infrastruktur fürs Radfahren, wollte ich schnell von A nach B kommen, war ich gezwungen, auf der Straße mitten zwischen den Autos zu fahren. Aber im Gegensatz zu den deutschen AutofahrerInnen, die mehrheitlich selbst Fahrrad fahren, in 80 Prozent der deutschen Haushalte existiert mindestens ein Fahrrad, waren die britischen AutolenkerInnen auf meine Anwesenheit auf der Straße nicht vorbereitet.

Ich geriet mehrfach in höchst gefährliche Situationen, fing dann an, auf Fußwegen zu fahren und war schnell mit ärgerlichen FußgängerInnen konfrontiert. Wiederholt erklärte ich ihnen, dass ich dies nur täte, weil die Straße zu gefährlich für mich sei und es keine Radwege gäbe, aber viel Verständnis habe ich nicht gefunden. Doch ich gab nicht auf, und mein Mann und ich riefen Ende 2004 die Darlington Cycling Campaign ins Leben. Heute hat die Kampagne mehr als 100 Mitglieder, und sie ist eine respektierte politische Stimme.

Zeitnah zur Gründung unserer Kampagnengruppe erhielt Darlington den Zuschlag des Department for Transport, des britischen Verkehrsministeriums, als eine von drei „Sustainable Travel Demonstration Towns" und von Cycling England, einer halböffentlichen Vereinigung aus London, als eine von sechs „Cycling Demonstration Towns". Insgesamt sollte Darlington mehr als sechs Millionen Pfund Sterling erhalten, um die Bedingungen für den Umweltverbund und insbesondere für die FahrradfahrerInnen zu verbessern. Seit Oktober 2005 gibt Darlington rund 10 Pfund pro Einwohner und Jahr für die Förderung des Radverkehrs aus.[1]

Das sind gute Voraussetzungen, um das Leben der RadfahrerInnen zu verbessern, den Autoverkehr

1   Vgl. Local Motion (Hrsg.): Cycling Town Review 2005/2009, Seite 3

zu reduzieren und damit die Lebensqualität in Darlington zu steigern. Natürlich kann in vier Jahren nicht die Welt verändert werden, kann nicht erwartet werden, dass plötzlich 25 Prozent aller Wege in Darlington auf dem Rad vollzogen werden. Doch trotz aller „natürlichen" Vorteile ihrer Stadt fahren auch nach fünf Jahren aktiver Förderung des Fahrradfahrens nur wenige Menschen Fahrrad, der Anteil des Rades an den in Darlington unternommenen Fahrten ist von 1 auf nur 3 Prozent angestiegen. Die Ergebnisse sind trotzdem bemerkenswert, denn der Anteil der Wege im Auto in Darlington ist um 6 Prozent gesunken, während 4 Prozent mehr Wege zu Fuß unternommen werden.[2]

Britische Mädchen fahren kaum Fahrrad

Beim Fahrradfahren ist auffällig, dass viel mehr Männer und Jungen Fahrrad fahren als Mädchen und Frauen: Die Fahrrad-Straßenszene wird beherrscht von Männern in Rennkleidung mit Helm und Lycra-Anzügen und Jungs auf BMX-Rädern oder Mountainbikes. Frauen gehen mehr zu Fuß (31 Prozent ihrer Wege) oder nehmen den Bus (11 Prozent), aber nur für 2 Prozent nehmen sie das Fahrrad, während Männer immerhin 5 Prozent ihrer Wege auf dem Rad zurücklegen.[3]

Ganz besonders alarmierend ist, dass in Darlington fast kein Mädchen, kein Teenager Fahrrad fährt. Und da steht Darlington nicht alleine da, in fast ganz Großbritannien sieht es so aus, die nationalen Statistiken sprechen traurige Bände: Mädchen zwischen 11 und 16 Jahren fahren im Durchschnitt 13-mal im Jahr Fahrrad, Jungen immerhin 46-mal. Das rutscht mit zunehmendem Alter weiter ab: Zwischen 17 und 20 Jahren fahren Mädchen nur 5-mal im Jahr durchschnittlich mit dem Rad, Jungen noch 29-mal.[4] Kinder benutzen ihre Räder lediglich als Spielzeuge, aber mit dem Heranwachsen hören sie damit weitgehend auf.

Zwar fahren mittlerweile – dank der britischen Förder- und Trainingsprogramme und hier insbesondere des Bike It Programms von Sustrans[5] – viel mehr Grundschulkinder in Darlington Fahrrad, durchschnittlich 6 Prozent dieser Altersgruppe. Aber bisher fahren diese Kinder kaum weiter Fahrrad, wenn sie mit 11 in die weiterführende Schule kommen.

In fahrradfreundlichen Städten auf dem europäischen Kontinent sieht das ganz anders aus: Je älter die Kinder werden, desto mehr fahren sie Fahrrad, eine logische Folge, denn ihre Schulwege werden länger. Es gibt einen Abfall der Zahlen, wenn die Jugendlichen ihren Führerschein machen und das Auto für sich entdecken. Aber der generelle Trend der Kinder und Jugendlichen ist erst

2   Darlington verfügt über exzellente Daten im Verkehrsbereich dank der Arbeit der Münchner Agentur Socialdata: Vgl. Socialdata/Sustrans (Hrsg.): Darlington – Sustainable Travel Demonstration Town. Travel Behaviour Research. Final evaluation report for Darlington Borough Council, March 2009, S. 19

3   Vgl. Socialdata: Darlington 2009, Tabelle 15

4   Vgl. Department for Transport (Hrsg.): National Statistics. Cycling. Personal Fact Travelsheet – January 2007

5   Vgl. www.sustrans.org.uk

a Sustrans-led "Bike It" programme to encourage cycling to school. Primary schools in particular have been successful in getting their pupils to cycle more. But as secondary schools have discovered, take up amongst older teenagers drops off rapidly, and especially amongst girls.

Intriguingly, the statistics in cycling-friendly towns and cities are just the opposite. As children become teenagers, they use the bicycle more and more, most especially when cycling to secondary school. Of course, at age 17/18, as young adults pass their driving tests, inevitably some switch to the car. But the general trend from childhood to teenage-hood is towards the bicycle. Moreover, there is no statistical difference in numbers of cyclists between girls and boys. [7] In Bremen, our own research at Obervieland School found more than 50% of boys and girls regularly cycling to school.

Why Do British Girls Stop Cycling when they Become Teenagers?

Why do children – human beings at the most active stage in their lives – prefer to walk, when a bicycle is much faster? Why do healthy grown-ups in many European towns and cities use a car for very short trips? Why do British girls and teenagers elsewhere in Europe stop cycling as soon as they reach their mid-teens – apart from rare exceptions? Has it something to do with their natural equipment? Are British, French, Italian, Polish or Spanish girls less active and sporty than Dutch, Danish or German teenagers?

On the other hand, why do girls (and boys) in other European towns and cities, in Groningen and Amsterdam, in Odense and Copenhagen and in Münster and Bremen cycle to school every day, cycle to university, to work, to the shops, to the disco in such large numbers? Is cycling not part of the genetic code of British girls?

Of course these explanations are ludicrous. Nobody is "born" with a tendency to cycle. There are variations in temperament, energy and physique amongst teenagers. But anyone who has ever seen the explosion of energetic power at the beginning of a school break, knows how strong the urge to be active is with kids. A healthy child or teenager wants to move, needs physical activity, be it a boy or a girl. So why do they seem to prefer a car to a bicycle? And if the car or the parental chauffeur is not available, why does the British kid prefer to walk rather than cycle? If it is not the genes, it must be the environment.

7   See Statistisches Bundesamt (Hrsg.): Verkehr in Deutschland 2006, Wiesbaden 2006 and Institut Wohnen und Umwelt, Planungsgemeinschaft Verkehr und Psychologisches Institut der TU Darmstadt (Hrsg.): Einflussgrößen und Motive der Fahrradnutzung im Alltagsverkehr, Abschlußbericht, Darmstadt/Hannover 2002, Institut Wohnen und Umwelt, Planungsgemeinschaft Verkehr (Hrsg.): Stadtbericht Bremen. Ergebnisse zum Projekt: Einflussgrößen und Motive der Fahrradnutzung im Alltagsverkehr, Darmstadt/Hannover Februar 2002

einmal Richtung Fahrrad. Und hier gibt es keine nennenswerten Unterschiede zwischen Mädchen und Jungen. [6]

Fehlt britischen Mädchen das Fahrrad-Gen?

Warum ziehen (britische) Kinder – Menschen im aktivsten Alter - es vor, zu Fuß zu gehen, wenn ein Fahrrad sehr viel schneller wäre? Warum benutzen gesunde Erwachsene in vielen Städten Europas ein Auto für Wege unter zwei Meilen bzw. drei Kilometern? Warum hören Mädchen in vielen Ländern Europas als Teenager auf Rad zu fahren - bis auf wenige Ausnahmen? Hat das etwas mit Naturkonstanten zu tun? Sind britische, französische, italienische, polnische oder spanische Mädchen weniger aktiv und sportlich als holländische, dänische oder deutsche Mädchen?

Auf der anderen Seite: Warum fahren Mädchen (und Jungen) in anderen europäischen Städten, in Groningen und Amsterdam, in Odense und Kopenhagen, in Münster und Bremen völlig selbstverständlich jeden Tag mit dem Rad zur Schule, zur Universität, zur Arbeit, zum Einkaufen, in die Disko oder wohin sie auch immer wollen? Fehlt den britischen Mädchen das „Fahrrad-Gen", heißt, anders gesagt: Holländerin sein, gleich Radfahrerin sein?

Alle diese Erklärungsversuche erscheinen schnell lächerlich, denn offensichtlich wird niemand mit dem Hang zum Fahrradfahren geboren genauso wenig wie niemand mit dem Lenkrad eines Autos in der Hand auf die Welt kommt. Es gibt Unterschiede im Temperament, im natürlichen Bewegungsdrang oder in der generellen Körperausstattung. Aber, wer einmal erlebt hat, mit welcher Explosion an Energie eine Pause in der Schule beginnt, wie Kinder nach ein oder zwei Schulstunden auf einen Schulhof stürmen, weiß, mit wie viel Bewegungsdrang das durchschnittliche Kind ausgestattet ist.

Ein gesundes Kind und ein normaler Teenager wollen sich bewegen. Warum „neigt" das britische Kind zum Auto? Und wenn das Auto (und die elterliche FahrerIn) nicht zur Verfügung steht, warum geht ein britisches Kind lieber zu Fuß als sich auf das schnellere und bequemere Fahrrad zu schwingen? Die Antwort kann nicht in den Genen liegen, und dann bleibt eigentlich nur die Umwelt, die Gesellschaft, die Umgebung.

---

6   Vgl. hierzu: Statistisches Bundesamt (Hrsg.): Verkehr in Deutschland 2006, Wiesbaden 2006 und Institut Wohnen und Umwelt, Planungsgemeinschaft Verkehr und Psychologisches Institut der TU Darmstadt (Hrsg.): Einflussgrößen und Motive der Fahrradnutzung im Alltagsverkehr, Abschlußbericht, Darmstadt/Hannover 2002, Institut Wohnen und Umwelt, Planungsgemeinschaft Verkehr (Hrsg.): Stadtbericht Bremen. Ergebnisse zum Projekt: Einflussgrößen und Motive der Fahrradnutzung im Alltagsverkehr, Darmstadt/Hannover Februar 2002

It's the Infrastructure, Stupid!

Many subjective reasons are given by teenage girls who do not cycle. "Not cool", "it's a kids' thing", "rain", "theft of bikes", "hills" were just some of them. But by comparing conditions in the UK with those in cycling-friendly towns and cities, many of these can be discounted as having no bearing on whether girls in general cycle or not. Rather, we found that the key differences between Darlington and Bremen girls lay in the material conditions in which they are expected to cycle, and the cultural consequences these conditions produced.

Subjective perceptions of cycling amongst teenage girls concentrate on the final outcome of this: peer group pressure and anxious parents. It is decidedly "uncool" to cycle amongst teenage girls. And parents see it as simply too dangerous to cycle. But, like Hegel versus Marx, it is a mistake to believe that these cultural attitudes shape a lack of cycling. Rather the material conditions offered to cycling in the UK shape these attitudes: It is obvious – not just in Britain but in many European countries – that there is something missing on the roads: cycling infrastructure. It is also missing in most places in France, Italy or Spain, but the Brits are most consistent in leaving it out. And typical for Britain, Darlington's roads are designed for car use. Lanes are generously wide in comparison to the minimum requirements of an urban main road [8], seducing car drivers into driving faster. Pavements are relatively narrow. At many junctions pedestrians are confronted with railings, herding them like sheep to one crossing point.

Roundabouts are most dangerous for the non-motorised. There are no precautions for cyclists, no priority for them at entries and exits. Roundabouts as a form of road infrastructure greatly favours motorised transport to the disadvantage of cyclists. It is no coincidence that the UK is one of the most roundabout-obsessed countries in Europe.

Where smaller roads join main roads, car drivers have priority over pedestrians and cyclists. Contrary to the Highway Code, pedestrians cannot expect priority if they are first on the road before a car arrives.

Yet this again is not a God-given condition. Motorists in cycling-friendly towns and cities typically behave much more tolerantly towards cyclists. Motorist behaviour is a product of the key material condition that shapes us all. It's the infrastructure, stupid.

Cars Must not be Touched

Like Motorist behaviour, infrastructure is not God-given, infrastructure is a classical state task, it is planned and built by the government, the town hall shapes public spaces. And if public space is geared only to the car and subsequently against the bicycle, it is not the responsibility of a single

8   The authors measured Woodland Road, one of Darlington's arterial roads, at one of its narrowest points. Parking is forbidden on most of its length. Lane width was 4.91m. The minimum requirement for an HGV on a 30mph road is 3.25m

It's the Infrastructure, Stupid!

Die Mädchen selbst geben eine Reihe von subjektiven Gründen an, warum sie nicht Fahrrad fahren: Es ist nicht cool, nicht schick, nur was für Kleinkinder, das Wetter ist zu schlecht, Fahrräder werden geklaut und vieles andere. All das könnten Mädchen aus Bremen auch sagen. Zugespitzt gesagt, glauben die Mädchen in Darlington, dass sie nicht Fahrrad fahren, weil ihre Jugendkultur, ihre Peer Group es nicht zulässt und die Eltern zu ängstlich sind, um sie aufs Fahrrad zu lassen. Aber der wesentliche Unterschied zwischen Bremen und Darlington liegt in den materiellen Verhältnissen. Und so ist auch wie schon im Gegensatz zwischen Hegel und Marx klar: Nicht die kulturellen Bedingungen, das was sich im Kopf abspielt, führt zum Nicht-Fahrradfahren, sondern die handfeste materielle Situation auf den Straßen formt die Ideen gegen das Fahrradfahren.

Denn, was ins Auge springt, ist etwas, was nicht da ist: Infrastruktur fürs Fahrrad. Sie fehlt auch in den meisten Städten Frankreichs, Spaniens oder Italiens, aber die BritInnen sind am konsequentesten beim Weglassen. Darlington ist eine typische englische Stadt, ein Beispiel britischer Verkehrspolitik der vergangenen 40 Jahre, eine so genannte autogerechte Stadt. Alle Straßen sind so konstruiert, dass sie vor allem für Autos nutzbar sind. Generell sind die Fahrspuren überbreit, sodass der Autoverkehr dazu verleitet wird, schneller zu fahren als innerörtlich erlaubt.[7] Die Fußwege sind relativ schmal und für RadfahrerInnen ist an Hauptverkehrsstraßen grundsätzlich keine eigene Infrastruktur vorgesehen, weder Radwege noch abgeteilte Radspuren auf den Straßen. Von RadfahrerInnen wird erwartet, dass sie auf der Straße fahren.
Am gefährlichsten sind die zahlreichen Kreisverkehre: Sie sehen keinerlei Vorrechte oder Vorfahrtsregelungen für RadfahrerInnen vor. Kreisverkehre dieser Art bevorzugen den Autoverkehr, und es ist kein Wunder, dass Großbritannien zu den Ländern in Europa gehört, die die meisten Kreisverkehre haben.

7   Wir haben Woodland Road, eine der Hauptverkehrsstraßen in Darlington, auf ihre Breite hin gemessen: An ihrer engsten Stelle (Parken ist auf dieser Straße weitgehend untersagt) misst eine Fahrspur 4,91 Meter. Für einen Lastwagen ist die Mindestbreite auf einer Straße mit einer Höchstgeschwindigkeit von 30 Meilen 3,25 Meter.

parent or a teenage girl. Responsible is the state, changes have to come from the town hall. A teenager cannot do that, even if she wants to.

But so far the "anti-cycling" nature of British roads is not obvious to British politicians. Quite the contrary: The unspoken rule amongst most politicians in Britain seems to be "do not touch car space". The open rule is still „Predict and Provide". Just a few years ago Darlington spent 12 Mio. pounds on a completely new road (with a lovely cycle path). Here cycling is supported not for transport policy reasons but for a better environment, and in Darlington's town hall few seem to believe that a clear pro-cycling policy even if it disadvantages cars can help to solve traffic problems. British road planners do not seem to see, that more cyclists on main roads can mean less cars and less congestion.

In Darlington, the council is developing advisory routes away from main roads, and green routes for leisure rides. All these routes mean deviations for cyclists, rather than for motorists. None involve a redistribution of road space away from cars and to cyclists. Rather, cyclists are asked to train on these quiet routes until they are fit enough to take up the fight with cars on main roads.

Such a policy has two outcomes for cyclists. If I want to travel free of heavy traffic, I need more time. But if I want to choose a direct route, I need more guts. If infrastructure had a voice, it would tell us that, with these policies, you need to make sacrifices to cycle, sacrifices in time, sacrifices in comfort, sacrifices in road space. Cycling becomes a 2nd class mode of transport, for the poor or the environmentally committed.

Problem: Behaviour of Car Drivers

Speed limits are a big debating point in the UK. Currently, many residents, and most cycling campaigns, want to see a 20mph speed limit in urban areas. Accidents to pedestrians and cyclists alike are strongly linked to high speed urban traffic. The irony, from a cyclist's point of view, is that generous road space for motor cars encourages such speeding. Yet cyclists are expected to share this space. The result is a constant negotiation between cars that want to travel faster, and cyclists who want to travel slower.

Thus, cyclists have difficulty overtaking parked cars because the traffic behind them does not allow them to move out. The same applies to potholes, turning right off a main road, or negotiating roundabouts. Even the simple act of overtaking a cyclist can be fraught with mis-judgement by the motorist. Add to this mix of over-generous infrastructure and cyclists the perceived status of cycling as 2nd class, and you can get some distinctly nasty behaviour:

"Last week James Martin, the television celebrity chef, described in a newspaper his joy at running a group of cyclists off the road and into a hedge while test-driving a sports car. Martin was forced to apologise after thousands of angry cyclists protested" And Mr. Martin is not alone: "Matthew Parris, a columnist for the The Times, was similarly forced to backtrack last year after suggesting

An Einmündungen von Nebenstraßen in Hauptstraßen wird dem Autoverkehr prinzipiell Vorfahrt vor FußgängerInnen und RadfahrerInnen gewährt. Selbst auf den wenigen Radwegen ist die RadlerIn an Kreuzungen mit dem roten Dreieck konfrontiert, das ihr explizit die Vorfahrt nimmt. Und sogar FußgängerInnen, die nach dem britischen Highway Code Vorfahrt haben, wenn sie sich bereits auf der Straße befinden, können sich nicht darauf verlassen, dass AutofahrerInnen dies beachten. Infrastruktur fällt jedoch nicht vom Himmel, und das Benehmen der AutofahrerInnen ist nur ein Ergebnis davon und damit veränderbar, wie das Verhalten der AutofahrerInnen in Bremen zeigt. Infrastruktur wird gebaut und zwar nicht von den einzelnen Menschen in ihren Siedlungen, vielmehr ist Infrastruktur eine klassische staatliche Aufgabe. Wie die öffentlichen Räume gestaltet werden, liegt in der Hand des Rathauses. Und ist diese Gestaltung ausschließlich autoorientiert und damit fahrradfeindlich, muss sich nicht die einzelne BürgerIn fragen, wo ihre Handlungsspielräume liegen, um die Straße menschenfreundlich zu gestalten. Die Verantwortung liegt bei der Politik, die Veränderung muss aus dem Rathaus kommen.

Politik tastet Autoinfrastruktur nicht an

Das Problem der Fahrradfeindlichkeit ihrer Infrastruktur ist von politischer Seite in Großbritannien offenbar noch nicht erkannt worden: Die Veränderung der vom Auto dominierten Infrastruktur steht bisher nicht zur Debatte. Noch gilt „predict and provide": Erst vor wenigen Jahren ist in Darlington mit 12 Millionen Pfund eine völlig neue Straße gebaut worden (mit einem wunderschönen Radweg). Das Fahrradfahren wird hier nicht aus verkehrspolitischen sondern aus umweltpolitischen Gründen gefördert, die möglichen Vorteile der offensiven und sogar gegen die Interessen der AutofahrerInnen gerichteten Transportpolitik scheinen ins Rathaus von Darlington noch nicht vorgedrungen zu sein. Dass mehr RadfahrerInnen auf Hauptverkehrsstraßen weniger Autos und damit weniger Staus bedeuten können, haben die britischen VerkehrsplanerInnen noch nicht verinnerlicht.

Keine der Maßnahmen der vergangenen Jahre, die den Umweltverbund fördern und Menschen aus dem Auto heraus bringen sollten, haben beim Autoverkehr irgendetwas grundsätzlich verändert. Es gibt kein Beispiel, in dem den Autos auch nur ein Meter an Fläche genommen worden wäre – bis auf die neue Fußgängerzone. Ausnahmen sind die wenigen Busspuren auf Hauptverkehrsstraßen, die Fahrräder auch nutzen dürfen, oder einige wenige Radwege an neuen Straßen. Bestehende Straßen wurden nicht angetastet. Die Politik bevorzugt die Ausweisung von Radrouten, weg von den Hauptverkehrsstraßen, die nicht nur einen Umweg bedeuten, sondern auch abends für Frauen nicht zumutbar sind, da sie durch einsame Gegenden, Grünanlagen oder Wege weg von den belebten Orten führen. Ebenso sind Tunnel unter Kreuzungen oder Kreiseln sehr beliebt bei den StraßenbauerInnen, für Frauen ist diese Verkehrsführung unzumutbar und mit Angst besetzt. Unsichere RadfahrerInnen sollen auf diesen Nebenrouten Selbstvertrauen üben, und es wird erwartet, dass sie später auf Hauptverkehrsstraßen mitten zwischen den Autos klarkommen.

that piano wire should be strong across roads to decapitate cyclists." [9]

It would seem that many car drivers believe that they do not have to abide by social laws. In fact they enjoy special rights, and not just in Britain, as the Austrian transport scientist Hermann Knoflacher points out. Motorists, he explains, are allowed to make more noise than anyone else, to pollute the environment and put other people in danger. A shouting drunkard will be arrested for the noise he makes, but car noise pollution is acceptable. If a pedestrian were to spray cancerous substances into the air, he would face serious legal problems. Meanwhile thousands of car drivers do that every day, shortening our life time by an average 12 years. [10]

This behaviour of car drivers in the UK is regarded as quite normal. But as someone who is used to much more consideration towards cyclists, it came as a great shock. From my perspective, such behaviour seems reckless and aggressive. My experience on the roads of Darlington is one of constant discomfort on main roads, knowing that I always have to be vigilant for poor motorist judgement. This is bad enough. But the classifying of cycling as 2nd class also gave me a taste of the James Martin School of bigotry towards cycling. I myself have had drivers shouting at me as they pass at speed. One of the Darlington girls was deliberately driven off the road by a white van driver, who then returned to laugh at her resultant fall (fortunately she was only grazed). And other girls report verbal abuse from passing motorists.

Dealing with this combination of speed and abuse as a cyclist is the stuff of cycling campaign legends. Many a joking debate has been had about the availability of anti-tank mines as a defence mechanism against the worst motorists. Going to work on a bicycle is a big fight against car drivers on main roads. And because of this, it is, after all, a serious sport, requiring considerable expenditure of adrenalin and energy. This is the stuff of machismo, cycling-style.

9   http://www.timesonline.co.uk/tol/news/politics/article6841326.ece?p...

10   Knoflacher, Hermann: Das Auto macht uns total verrückt. Wir legen immer größere Distanzen zurück, um dieselben Bedürfnisse zu befriedigen. In: Die Zeit Nr. 38 aus 2007, S. 26. http://www.zeit.de/2007/38/Interv_-Knoflacher

Die Folgen für den Radverkehr sind augenfällig. Will ich als Radfahrerin sicher von A nach B kommen, kann ich nicht die schnellste Verbindung wählen, das wäre die Hauptverkehrsstraße, sondern ich muss mir eine Route überlegen, die über kleinere, weniger befahrene Straßen führt. Ich bin immer gezwungen, einen längeren Weg in Kauf zu nehmen. Die Vorteile des Fahrrades werden damit drastisch eingeschränkt. Es bleibt unter diesen Umständen ein Verkehrsmittel, das mühsamer und langsamer ist als das Auto. Alltägliches Radfahren ist damit mehr eine Opfergabe an die Umwelt als dass das Rad ein praktisches und komfortables Verkehrsmittel wäre.

Verhalten der AutofahrerInnen: Die Straße mutiert zum rechtsfreien Raum

Diese Art der Verkehrsführung hat unweigerlich Folgen: Der Autoverkehr versammelt alle Privilegien auf seiner Seite, und grundsätzlich wird in Darlington viel zu schnell gefahren. Und kaum eine AutofahrerIn hat Respekt vor schwächeren VerkehrsteilnehmerInnen oder nimmt Rücksicht auf sie. AutofahrerInnen verstoßen tagtäglich gegen die Regeln des Highway Codes, das Auto nimmt das Recht des Stärkeren für sich in Anspruch.

Die Straße tendiert damit, zum rechtsfreien Raum zu verkommen: Denn das Auto versucht, seine Geschwindigkeit durchzusetzen. Das Fahrrad ist jedoch zweifellos langsamer, und der motorisierte Verkehr ist nicht bereit, sich auf diese unterschiedlichen Geschwindigkeiten einzustellen. Deswegen werden Fahrräder auf Hauptverkehrsstraßen wie Luft behandelt: So können FahrradfahrerInnen nur schwer an parkenden Autos vorbei fahren, weil der hinter ihnen fließende Verkehr sie nicht ausscheren lässt. Das Gleiche gilt für Schlaglöcher, auch hier muss sich das Fahrrad den Weg um das Schlagloch erkämpfen, die Antwort des Autos ist oft ein wütendes Hupen hinter dem Fahrrad.

But for the typical teenage girl, this world is distinctly unattractive. How can you relax on a bicycle in these conditions? The joy of cycling dies out. I sometimes feel like I've been beamed back to the Wild West, but without my colt. Is it any wonder then that young people aim to be a car driver as soon as possible, to become a first class human being, to achieve all the privileges car drivers get on the roads? And that as an interim solution, since cycling is too dangerous, walking gives you less stress?

This mix of low status and road danger in comparison to driving manifests itself in the way teenagers do, or do not, cycle in the UK. Anxiety and being treated like 2nd class can easily be packed into the concept of cycling being "not cool". Subsequently boys on BMX or mountain bikes will typically, to the annoyance of adults, use the pavement. Ironically this, rather than dangerous motoring, is regarded as anti-social behaviour. But that does not appeal to most girls. And as the peer group opposes cycling and calls it "not cool" girls do not cycle.

Peer Group: There is no Escape from Your Clique

This became clear to me: It is the conservative attitude of peer groups, that keeps British teenagers and girls in particular, away from cycling. "Innovations" like cycling are not seen as fitting into the overall youth group system and most young people, ill at ease with their sense of self anyway, are not interested in experiencing new things. One girl – a keen cyclist - explained it to me: "I think the bike thing is just such a new concept to all groups. They are all very confused at first and are not brave enough to try it themselves, as they may be judged by the rest of their group. I think that the bikes (the Dutch bikes, B.W.) are so unusual, which also adds to that fact."

A girl riding a Dutch bike does not fit into any youth group, and without a group you are lost. The girl described it very neatly: "Groups exist across the UK, and they all know what they want and what they have to do to 'survive' in these groups. It's crazy but that's how it is. Teenagers are very, very strong minded in this way and these groups don't like something new and different most of the time. So for example if a Goth started riding a motorbike, it would be very abnormal, so they would most likely be picked on for that. Fashion and style do come into it, but there are the other elements too. To be socially accepted you cannot really live as a teenager without being categorised into a group! You tend to always have a group no matter what. If you don't think you are in a group you will be, as other groups will have a 'group' for you."

And whilst in bicycle friendly cities like Bremen teenagers find it annoying, when a member of their peer group does not have a bike, it is exactly the other way round in Darlington. "Cycling is not seen as stylish, it does not appeal to girls", was the explanation I got from girls in Darlington. These girls - working with us on our project - were eventually all cycling, and their parents were cycling as well. But most British parents do not want to put themselves in danger, do not cycle, and they do not want their kids to do so.

Wie Überholmanöver sind auch Richtungsänderungen, also rechts abbiegen nahezu unmöglich. Auf normaler Strecke überholen Autos mit hoher Geschwindigkeit und sehr nah und oft unnötig, nämlich noch kurz bevor diese Autos abbiegen. In Kreisverkehren ist das Problem noch größer. Sie werden von den AutofahrerInnen zum Beschleunigen genutzt. Vereinzelt auftretende RadlerInnen werden ignoriert, und beim Herausfahren aus dem Kreisel können immer wieder Autos beobachtet werden, die der RadfahrerIn rigoros die Vorfahrt abschneiden, sie zur Vollbremsung zwingen.

Bedrückend ist aber die auch öffentlich geäußerte Einstellung von Prominenten, die eigentlich als Vorbilder dienen sollten: „Last week James Martin, the television celebrity chef, described in a newspaper his joy at running a group of cyclists off the road and into a hedge while test-driving a sports car." Noch bunter trieb es Matthew Parris, ein Korrespondent der Times, der 2008 vorschlug, doch Klaviersaiten über Straßen zu spannen, um RadfahrerInnen zu enthaupten.[8] Offenbar glauben sich AutofahrerInnen im Auto den gesellschaftlichen Regeln enthoben: Sie genießen nach Auffassung des österreichischen Verkehrswissenschaftlers Hermann Knoflacher sogar so etwas wie Rechtsfreiheit und das beileibe nicht nur in Großbritannien. „Im Gegensatz zu allen anderen Menschen dürfen sie die Umwelt straffrei verlärmen, verunreinigen und die öffentliche Sicherheit gefährden."[9]

Dieses Verhalten hat nun allerdings nicht unbedingt etwas mit männlichem Dominanzgehabe zu tun, auch Frauen fahren rücksichtslos Auto in Großbritannien. Wer wie ich an andere Bedingungen und Autofahrerverhalten gewöhnt ist, fragt sich unwillkürlich: Warum verhalten sich rationale, gut erzogene Menschen in ihrem Auto wie die Rüpel? Mit ein wenig Nachdenken und Beobachten ist die Antwort ganz einfach: It's the infrastructure, stupid!

RadfahrerInnen sind Menschen zweiter Klasse

Fahrradfahren auf solchen Straßen mit solchen infrastrukturellen Bedingungen und solchem Autobenehmen ist unattraktiv, weil unbequem und gefährlich. Wenn dann noch offene Diskriminierung dazu kommt, wenn Frauen auf Fahrrädern von Männern in Autos angeherrscht und angemacht werden, wenn Autofahrer junge Mädchen absichtlich in Gefahr bringen, hört der Spaß vollständig auf. Denn so unglaublich das für eine BremerIn klingt: Genau damit muss sie auf den Straßen von Darlington tagtäglich rechnen. Ich persönlich fühle mich hier auf meinem Fahrrad wie im Wilden Westen nur ohne Revolver.

---

8   Vgl. http://www.timesonline.co.uk/tol/news/politics/article6841326.ece?p...

9   Knoflacher, Hermann: Das Auto macht uns total verrückt. Wir legen immer größere Distanzen zurück, um dieselben Bedürfnisse zu befriedigen. In: Die Zeit Nr. 38 aus 2007, S. 26. http://www.zeit.de/2007/38/Interv -Knoflacher : „Ein randalierender Betrunkener wird wegen Lärmbelästigung verhaftet, Autofahrer, die zu allen Tages- und Nachtzeiten unsere Häuser beschallen, werden akzeptiert. Würde ich als Fußgänger mit einer Dose krebserregende Substanzen versprühen, wäre das gesetzeswidrig. Tausende Autofahrer tun das täglich ungehindert und verkürzen die Lebenszeit von uns allen um durchschnittlich zwölf Jahre."

Parenting: The Missing Role Model

For children, adults are their natural role models and most kids adopt their parents' every day habits. Adult assumptions about how to get from A to B, inevitably shapes their kids' attitudes towards their own mobility. If it is seen as normal that dad drives round the corner to get his newspaper, then the kids will internalise this. If he uses his bicycle for these errands, then a daughter might cycle to the shop for her sweets as well.

Today, British kids live in a thoroughly motorised society. A tiny minority have parents that cycle, even fewer who use their bike as a normal everyday means of transport. Women on bicycles are rarer still, especially on main roads. You might find some at weekends, out with their families on a leisure ride. On average, women cycle just 13 trips per year. More than two thirds of the whole population (69 percent) - women and men, mothers and fathers - never use a bike, or use one less than once a year.[11] Nowhere is this fact more acutely felt than on the infamous school run.

A child's mobility is always shaped by elements of playing. If you have ever carefully watched a primary school kid on its way to school, you will have seen that this child is constantly discovering something. It finds a stone; it sees a new flower, talks to the post woman, uses its stone to paint a wall in passing and tosses it away again. Dawdling children do not dawdle in an adult sense. They are in fact very busy watching, trying, dreaming and communicating.

In Bremen, the majority of children manage to get to school without parents from their first year. Many of them use their little bicycles, riding on the pavement or cycle path, mostly in groups, their schoolbags on their back or tied to the luggage rack. They ride in wavy lines, they arrange little races, or they just cycle side by side and talk incessantly. After school, they meet with their friends on the roads, on the playgrounds or in a park.

11   See for these figures: Department for Transport (Ed.): National Statistics: Travel to Work. Personal Travel Fact Sheet – July 2007, Transport: Cycling 2007 and Socialdata: Darlington 2009

Die RadfahrerIn wird zum Menschen zweiter Klasse degradiert, und die fatale Schlussfolgerung von Jugendlichen ist: Ich muss so schnell wie möglich eine AutofahrerIn werden, dann bin ich Mensch erster Klasse, kriege ich alle die Auto-Privilegien zugestanden. Die zweite ist eine Interimslösung: Das Fahrradfahren ist mir zu gefährlich, ich gehe zu Fuß, da habe ich weniger Stress.

Die alltägliche Bedrohung von RadfahrerInnen auf britischen Straßen führt natürlich zu schwarzem Humor in Fahrradgruppen: So wird auf manchen Treffen diskutiert, ob es vielleicht auf dem Schwarzmarkt noch alte Anti-Panzer-Minen aus dem Zweiten Weltkrieg gibt, die gegen allzu rabiate Autofahrerinnen einsetzbar wären. Unter diesen schwierigen Bedingungen wird Fahrradfahren wieder zum schweißtreibenden Sport, wer mit dem Rad zur Arbeit fährt, braucht eine Dusche, das ist eine Sache für ganze Männer: Fahrradmachismo treibt seine munteren Blüten.

Das Ergebnis ist nicht verwunderlich: Mädchen fahren nicht Fahrrad. Und es ist auch nicht erstaunlich, dass der Rest der Jugendlichen keine Lust auf ein Verkehrsmittel hat, das mit so viel Risiko verbunden ist. In Verbrämung der nicht eingestandenen Angst wird Fahrradfahren kurzerhand für uncool erklärt. Die so genannten Peer Groups erlauben es deswegen nicht. Und das ist noch ein Grund für die Mädchen gegen das Rad.

Druck aus der Peer Group: Niemand entrinnt dem Cliquensystem

„Neuerungen" wie das Fahrradfahren gelten in der Jugendkultur von Darlington nicht als konform. In einem Gespräch hat mir das ein Mädchen, das selbst gerne Fahrrad fährt, erklärt : "I think the bike thing is just such a new concept to all groups so they are all very confused at first and are not brave enough to try it themselves at first, as they may be judged by the rest of their group. I think that the bikes (Hollandräder, B.W.) are so unusual which also adds to that fact."

Mit einem Stadtrad oder Hollandrad passt kein Mädchen in eine Gruppe, und ohne Gruppe ist das Leben schwer: "Groups exist across the UK and they all know what they want and what they have to do to 'survive' in these groups. (...) To be socially accepted you cannot really live as a teenager without being categorised into a group! You tend to always have a group no matter what. If you don't think you are in a group, you will be as other groups will have a 'group' for you."

Und während in fahrradfreundlichen Städten wie Bremen es die Jugendlichen nervig finden, wenn ein Mitglied in ihrer Gruppe kein Fahrrad hat, ist es in Darlington genau anders herum. Radfahren gilt nicht als schick, nicht als „stylish", „it does not appeal to girls", „es spricht Mädchen nicht an" war die Erklärung meiner jungen Gesprächspartnerin.

In Darlington, every morning at a quarter to nine, a car procession develops in front of every school. This parade of teachers, mothers and fathers leads to congestion in front of the schools. Half an hour later all the cars vanish, to return in the afternoon at 3:15 p.m.. More than a third of all primary school kids in Darlington are ferried to school with a car, and at some schools this proportion increases to 70%. The rest walk, most of them accompanied by an adult. On average only 6% cycle.

If parents do not cycle, if they use a car for even the shortest trips, if they ferry their kids to school from the beginning and even do so after school in leisure times, under these conditions a child is educated into the role of a car child. "I need a lift" is a frequent refrain, and parents feel guilty if they do not grant this wish; indeed, they would see themselves as bad parents. Traffic is too dangerous to do otherwise. But a car-centric society is a privatised society. That car-driving parents themselves help create that danger is either not recognised, or leads to a culture of individual helplessness. Such problems need collective, community solutions.

Parenting: Overprotection

It is striking that children in Britain grow up much more protected and guarded than in Germany, reflecting different wider attitudes towards parenting. Parents do not seem to have a great belief in their kids' abilities. My experience in Darlington suggests that, if children are late for school, parents will frequently jump into their car and ferry them. They do not give their youngster a chance to experience the consequences of its own behaviour, of being late for school. But if mums or dads always volunteer to help out, a young person's sense of responsibility could take a long time to develop.

In my family there was an unspoken rule: I was responsible for getting to school on time. There would be no emergency ferry services just because I was too slow or sleepy and dragged my feet. This was one of the reasons I fought for a bike. Of course my parents would talk to me about dangers and tricky situations, but they would not build any defences around me, they would let me live my own experiences.

To most British parents, their children need protection from the "hostile environment" that lies outside the home – or the car. Because of all their cars, cycling is deemed to be extremely dangerous. Yet paradoxically, it would help their children if they were allowed to cycle. Children who go to school on their own from an early age have a better sense of orientation and more self confidence. Moreover, a human being on a bike is more aware of his or her environment than somebody sitting in a car. New and unexpected things are happening all the time, which touches the natural sense of curiosity in children; they have to deal with the world around them and can also live their natural tendency to play. A child without a bicycle grows up under more control and protection, but also with more restrictions.

Eltern bieten keine Vorbilder: Fahrrad ist kein Alltagsgerät

Die britischen Kinder heute erleben eine durchweg motorisierte Gesellschaft, nur wenige haben Eltern, die Fahrrad fahren, und schon gar nicht Eltern, die ein Fahrrad als tägliches normales Transportmittel nutzen. Und wenn es Fahrräder in einer Familie gibt, dann werden sie von den Jungen und Männern gefahren. Fahrradfahren in Großbritannien ist eine maskuline Fortbewegungsart: Frauen auf Rädern kommen auf Hauptverkehrsstraßen faktisch nicht vor. Sie finden sich am Wochenende mit der Familie auf Radrouten im Grünen, als Alltagsgerät nutzen sie ihr Fahrrad nicht. In keiner Altersgruppe fahren Frauen mehr als durchschnittlich 13 Wege pro Jahr mit dem Fahrrad. Mehr als zwei Drittel der Gesamtbevölkerung benutzt ein Fahrrad gar nicht oder weniger als ein Mal pro Jahr.[10]

Das Ergebnis ist so simpel wie bestürzend: Für britische Kinder gibt es fast keine elterlichen Vorbilder auf dem Fahrrad. Ein Marsmensch mit stromlinienförmigem Helm, „Insektenbrille" und gelber Plastikbekleidung, der schwitzend versucht, 30 oder 40 Meilen in der Stunde zu fahren, ist etwas zum Angucken aber nicht zum Mitmachen – das trifft vor allem auch für Mädchen zu. Kinder möchten spielen, nicht Leistungssport betreiben. Kindliche Mobilität hat immer etwas Spielerisches. Wer einmal ein Kind auf dem Weg zur Schule beobachtet hat, wird gesehen haben, dass es beständig dabei ist, etwas zu entdecken. Es findet einen Stein, es sieht eine neue Blume, unterhält sich mit dem Postboten, bemalt im Vorübergehen eine Wand mit seinem Stein, wirft ihn wieder weg. Trödelnde Kinder trödeln eben nicht im Erwachsenensinne, sie sind beschäftigt, mit Beobachten, Ausprobieren und Kommunizieren.

In Bremen gehen die meisten Kinder ab der ersten Klasse alleine oder mit anderen Kindern zur Schule, viele fahren mit ihren Kinderrädern auf dem Fußweg oder Fahrradweg, meistens fahren sie in Gruppen. Sie fahren Schlangenlinien, sie veranstalten kleine Rennen, oder sie fahren einfach nebeneinander her und reden.

In Darlington dagegen baut sich morgens um viertel vor neun vor jeder Schule ein Autokorso auf. Die Mütter-Väter-Parade verstopft den Straßenraum vor der Schule. Nach einer halben Stunde ist der Spuk vorbei, um sich ab 15:15 Uhr – denn um 15:30 Uhr ist Schulschluss – zu wiederholen. Die Statistik der Stadtverwaltung bestätigt das: Mehr als ein Drittel aller Kinder im Grundschulalter werden zur Schule gefahren, an manchen Schulen steigt dieser Anteil auf über 70 Prozent.

Wenn die Eltern nicht Fahrrad fahren, wenn sie fast alle, auch die kurzen Wege mit dem Auto unternehmen, ihre Kinder von der ersten Klasse an mit dem Auto zur Schule bringen und sie auch in der Freizeit herum chauffieren, wird das Kind zu einem Autokind erzogen: „Fährst Du mich?" ist dann zwangsläufig eine häufig gestellte Frage, und die Eltern haben ein schlechtes Gewissen, wenn sie diese Forderung nicht erfüllen, sie halten sich dann für schlechte Eltern.

10   Vgl. zu den Zahlen Department for Transport (Hrsg.): National Statistics: Travel to Work. Personal Travel Factsheet – July 2007 und Cycling 2007, Socialdata: Darlington 2009

"Cycling has four main attractions for children. First, it is great fun. Its combination of difficulty, self-directness and speed give it strong appeal. Second it has the potential to dramatically expand the territory over which children can get around. Trips too far, tiring or boring to complete on foot become straightforward, quick and fun by cycle. Third, cycling is usually a social activity, allowing children and young people to meet their friends, to travel around with them and to share the enjoyment of their activity. Fourth, cycling, like walking, allows for close engagement and interaction with the people, places and objects encountered en route – much more so than travelling by car." [12]

Of course the dangers for a child on a bike are higher than for the same kid at home or in the garden. It can hurt itself, but that is no reason to keep these experiences away from it. "A child who cycles is almost certain to sustain at least slight injuries as a result of learning and pursuing the activity. (...) Cycling feels dangerous partly because it involves speed and skill: unlike walking, cycling does not come naturally, and learning to cycle involves significant risk of accidents and injuries. Moreover in road environments cycling puts riders in close proximity to motor vehicles, which are obvious hazards and may feel especially threatening to inexperienced cyclists.(...) Indeed cycling is a good example of an activity where the single-minded pursuit of injury prevention at the expense of wider goals and benefits would, if taken to its logical conclusion, lead to its blanket prohibition." [13]

Cycling obviously gives young people independence from parents and elder siblings. A bicycle is cheap to use, with few repairs it is always available, and unlike timetable-restricted public transport, it can be used at all hours. In our project, we have learnt how important the role of parents is for the development of a young person's mobility. Most of the girls' parents encouraged their daughters to cycle, cycled with them, and helped them look after their bikes. They helped them to stand up to the social hostility they experienced when they first began cycling.

12   Gill, Tim: Cycling and Children and Young People. A Review. National Children's Bureau (Ed.), London, December 2005, p. 9
13   Gill: Children 2005, p. 9 and 29

Eltern überbehüten ihre Kinder

Immer wieder ist mir aufgefallen, dass Kinder in Großbritannien sehr viel behüteter und auch überwachter aufwachsen als etwa in Deutschland. Das ist im Wesentlichen eine Frage der grundsätzlichen Einstellung gegenüber Kindern und Jugendlichen. Britische Eltern scheinen ihren Kindern wenig Eigenverantwortung zuzutrauen. Ein Beispiel ist der morgendliche Ablauf: Trödelt das Kind oder die Jugendliche, springen die Eltern schnell mit dem Auto ein. Sie lassen ihren Kindern keine Möglichkeit, die Konsequenzen der Folgen des Zuspätkommens zu erleben, und Eigenverantwortung kann sich so nur schlecht entwickeln.

Bei uns in der Familie gab es eine unausgesprochene Regel: Für das Pünktlich sein bin ich selbst verantwortlich, Nottransporte mit dem Auto, nur weil ich getrödelt habe, gibt es nicht. Schon auch deswegen kämpfte ich früh für ein Fahrrad. Es war meinen Eltern wichtig, dass ich unabhängig von ihnen von A nach B kam. Natürlich wurde ich auf mögliche Gefahren hin gewiesen, aber es wurden keine Zäune um mich gebaut, sie ließen mich meine Erfahrungen machen.

Die meisten britischen Eltern dagegen glauben, ihren Kindern etwas Gutes zu tun, wenn sie sie behüten, begleiten und sie vor der „feindlichen Umwelt" abschirmen. Das Recht auf die eigene Gefahr, auf das eigene Risiko, auf das eigene Erleben von unangenehmen oder gefährlichen Situationen wird den Kindern nicht oder nur selten zugestanden. Und Fahrradfahren wird als besonders gefährlich angesehen – aufgrund von einer Verkehrssituation, die diese Erwachsenen selbst schaffen, für die alle Erwachsenen die Verantwortung tragen.

Trotz dieser Gefahren, wäre es wichtig, wenn die Kinder radeln dürften, denn Kinder, die schon früh alleine mit dem Rad gefahren sind, können sich besser orientieren und sind dadurch selbstbewusster. Ein Mensch auf dem Fahrrad nimmt seine Umwelt intensiver wahr als jemand in einem Auto. Neue, unerwartete Dinge passieren die ganze Zeit, das berührt die natürliche Neugier von Kindern, sie müssen sich mit der Umwelt auseinander setzen und können andererseits ihren Spieltrieb ausleben. Ein Kind ohne Fahrrad wächst kontrollierter, behüteter aber eben auch eingeschränkter auf, seine Entwicklung kann unter dieser Einengung leiden. Ein Kind im Auto muss die Welt passiv erleben. Natürlich besteht die Gefahr, dass es sich mit dem Fahrrad auch mal verletzt, aber das sollte kein Grund sein, seinem Kind diese Erfahrungen von Freiheit nicht zu gönnen.[11]

Auf der anderen Seit stellt sich für mich auch als Stiefmutter die Frage, warum es Kindern und Jugendlichen zugemutet wird, mit einer gefährlichen Infrastruktur zu leben, warum sie zum Fahrradfahren aufgefordert werden, ohne dass die wesentlichen Gefahrenpunkte fürs Fahrrad abgebaut werden. Warum erkennt eine rationale und dem Gemeinsinn verpflichtete Politik das Problem nicht? Es ist, als hätte die britische Verkehrspolitik – und nicht nur die britische – hier einen blinden Fleck. Und das ist befremdlich vor dem Hintergrund, dass die britische Gesellschaft das Thema Gefahrenabwehr nach außen hin als außerordentlich wichtig darstellt.

11 Vgl. Gill, Tim: Cycling and Children and Young People. A Review. Herausgegeben vom National Children's Bureau, London, Dezember 2005

But our project only touched a tiny minority of teenage girls. Perhaps they are the rebellious ones, the ones that are willing to challenge society's norms. Perhaps their parents are likewise willing to challenge orthodoxy. But for most Darlington parents, initiatives like "Safe Routes to School", "Bike It" or "Bikeability" are not persuasive enough in themselves as long as the infrastructure remains dangerous for cyclists.

As a step-parent myself, I ask myself, why children are asked to cycle in a dangerous environment, why children are talked into cycling, without taking away the main sources of danger in the first place? Why are politicians, rational and dedicated to the welfare of their community, so reluctant to make infrastructure actually attractive to cyclists – and genuinely safe for children? Here is the final barrier to a cycling-friendly society – the hypocrisy of risk assessment.

Risk in a Car Oriented Society: Dangers from Cars are Ignored

During my stays in Britain I discovered two peculiar social strands: paranoia towards risk and danger, and obsession with so called anti-social behaviour. In Britain everyone is accustomed to "Health and Safety" and "Risk Assessment". And the Blair administration initiated a campaign against anti-social behaviour in the 90s. Darlington has even set up an "Anti-Social Behaviour Team" to gather the complaints of its citizens. Every Darlingtonian is asked to report about incidents. But it is unclear what a good citizen is supposed to report in the first place. The British Home Secretary gives us a definition: "Anti-social behaviour is virtually any intimidating or threatening activity that scares you or damages your quality of life."[14] Does that also include the behaviour of car drivers?

Ask anyone in Britain who they see as the main instigators of anti-social behaviour, and most will point to young male citizens of the lower working class: the Chavs. Young men cycling on pavements is regarded by many in Darlington as an example of anti-social behaviour. But reckless behaviour of car drivers like driving too fast, ignoring cyclists' rights of way at junctions or on roundabouts, or cutting cyclists on overtaking? Not acceptable, perhaps, but not anti-social.

CCTV cameras are used extensively in the UK to monitor the activities of young people. A group of lads on BMXs in Darlington town centre are in themselves reason enough to attract the attention of CCTV operatives, whatever they are doing. This same technology was monitored over a 3 day period in 2007 by Darlington Cycling Campaign to show that, contrary to the calls from anti-cyclists, allowing cycling in the town's pedestrianised centre posed no significant risks . How technology is used is a political question. And politicians have been very choosy about which risks get assessed. With all the CCTV cameras they could easily assess the risks that cars impose on pedestrians and cyclists at junctions and on roundabouts and what has to be done to minimise these risks.[15]

Instead, health and safety, as it impinges on cyclists, almost inevitably leads to the question of hel-

14   See http://www.homeoffice.gov.uk/anti-social-behaviour/what-is-asb/
15   See http://bikedarlington.blogspot.com/2008/11/cycling-in-pedestrian-heart.html

Fragwürdige Einstellung zum Thema Gefahr in einer autoorientierten Gesellschaft: Ausblenden der Gefahr durchs Auto

Im Laufe meiner Zeit in Großbritannien ist mir aufgefallen, dass die britische Gesellschaft ein fast paranoid zu erscheinendes Verhältnis zum Thema Gefahr sowie anti-sozialem Verhalten hat: „Health and Safety" und „Risk Assessment", also: Gesundheit und Sicherheit sowie Gefahrenabschätzung sind Begriffe, die in Großbritannien nahezu jedes Kind kennt. Die Blair Regierung hatte außerdem die Bekämpfung des so genannten anti-sozialen Verhaltens auf ihre Fahnen geschrieben. Darlington hat im Herbst 2009 sogar ein „Anti-Social Behaviour Team" aufgestellt, das sich um Beschwerden der BürgerInnen und um Brennpunktgebiete kümmern soll.

Nach herrschender Auffassung (des britischen Innenministeriums) ist jedes einschüchternde oder gefährdende Verhalten anti-sozial, das einem anderen Menschen Angst macht oder seine Lebens-qualität einschränkt.[12] Gehört dazu auch das Verhalten des Autoverkehrs? Offenbar nicht, denn auffallend ist, dass dieser Begriff fast immer nur auf männliche Jugendliche der Unterschicht, hier Chavs genannt, angewendet wird. Aber rücksichtsloses, ja gesetzeswidriges Verhalten des motorisierten Verkehrs wie: zu schnelles Fahren, Abschneiden der Vorfahrt von RadfahrerInnen an Einmündungen und im Kreisverkehr und Abdrängen auf Hauptverkehrsstraßen gilt nicht als anti-sozial, höchstens als „nicht-akzeptabel".

Fast jedes Haus in diesem Land hat eine Alarmanlage, einmal in der Woche geht in unserer Straße eine defekte Anlage los. Und fast überall im öffentlichen Raum gibt es Überwachungskameras. Die Darlington Cycling Campaign hat diese Kameras in 2007 dafür genutzt, um nachzuweisen, dass Radfahren in der neuen Fußgängerzone keine Gefahr für die FußgängerInnen bedeutet.[13] Anders-

---

12   Vgl. http://www.homeoffice.gov.uk/anti-social-behaviour/what-is-asb/ „Anti-social behaviour is virtually any intimidating or threatening activity that scares you or damages your quality of life. "

13   Vgl. http://bikedarlington.blogspot.com/2008/11/cycling-in-pedestrian-heart-talking.html

mets. The debate about helmets is one of the UK's hobby horses. Who should wear a helmet, only kids or also adults? How safe is a helmet, does it protect from severe injuries or save my life? Or can we also receive injury through rotational forces or even strangulate ourselves? Does the helmet make a cyclist take more risks and seduce car drivers into treating cyclists less carefully? [16]

Of course, cycling can be a sport, where cyclists reach speeds of more than 40mph. Racing cyclists speed very closely together, and a helmet is more than reasonable in that situation. But if I cycle at 10mph, if I can stop very quickly, if my feet can reach the ground immediately, where is the danger? What the discussion about helmets conceals, is the fact that cyclists wear helmets to protect themselves from cars. The risk is not with the cyclist, but comes from the car driver. A logical step to help the cyclist would be to defuse the source of the danger. Strict speed limits, no priorities over cyclists and pedestrians and cycle paths, tracks or lanes on main roads. British politicians seem not to want to get involved in this problem. They fear for their votes at the next election, if they impose "unpopular" measures like reducing parking space or redistributing road space towards sustainable transport modes.

The girls in our project, on returning from Bremen to Darlington, found ways of overcoming many of the barriers that once prevented them from cycling. They used the Beauty and the Bike project as a means of forming new friendships, strong enough to resist peer group pressures. Their parents gave them vital support when they returned home after abuse on the town's roads. They developed their own sense of bike fashion, establishing an avant garde in Darlington rarely seen outside the big cities. But the infrastructure is something that, so far, they have been unable to sort out, at least alone. So most of the girls have joined Darlington Cycling Campaign.

16   See for this discussion: Gill: Children 2005, p. 31ff

herum könnte genauso ein Schuh daraus werden: Die Kameras an Kreisverkehren und Hauptverkehrsstraßen könnten schnell nachweisen, wie gefährlich der Autoverkehr für RadfahrerInnen ist und was verändert werden müsste.

Das wird jedoch nicht getan, stattdessen wird mit Inbrunst eine Debatte über das Helmtragen auf dem Rad geführt: Wer sollte einen Helm tragen, nur Kinder oder auch Erwachsene? Wie sicher ist ein Helm, verhindert er schwere Verletzungen oder Todesfälle? Können Helme auch schwere Drehverletzungen der Halswirbelsäule verursachen oder in unglücklichen Fällen zur Strangulation führen? Macht das Helmtragen die RadfahrerIn unvorsichtiger und führt dazu, dass AutofahrerInnen weniger vorsichtig mit RadfahrerInnen umgehen?[14]

Natürlich kann das Fahrradfahren Sport sein, die Tour de France ist ein Rennen, bei dem Geschwindigkeiten von mehr als 70 km/h erreicht werden können. Die Fahrer rasen auf engstem Raum neben-, vor- und hintereinander her, ein Helm macht hier Sinn. Aber wenn ich bei 15 km/h über eine glatte Strecke fahre, jederzeit anhalten kann, meine Füße sofort den Boden erreichen und mich abfangen können, wo ist die Gefahr?

Was die Helmdebatte verschweigt: FahrradfahrerInnen tragen Helme nicht, weil sie Angst haben, vom Rad zu fallen – diese Angst trifft höchstens für AnfängerInnen und Kinder zu - sondern um sich vor dem Autoverkehr zu schützen. Denn das Risiko des Fahrradfahrens liegt beim Auto und seiner FahrerIn. Angesichts dieser Lage rund ums Auto wäre die logische Konsequenz die Entschärfung der Gefahrenquelle Auto: Schärfere Tempolimits, keine Prioritäten und keine Vorfahrt für Autos gegenüber schwächeren VerkehrsteilnehmerInnen an Kreuzungen und Kreisverkehren und separate Führung des Radverkehrs auf Hauptverkehrsstraßen. Das alles passiert jedoch nicht.

Die Gefahrendebatte wird allerorts geführt, anti-soziales Verhalten soll bekämpft werden, aber nicht dort, wo es nötig wäre, beim Autoverkehr und der Verkehrsinfrastruktur: Es sieht so aus, als wolle die Politik sich damit nicht auseinander setzen, als wolle sie sich nicht mit den scheinbar so mächtigen AutofahrerInnen anlegen. Fürchten sie um die nächsten Wahlen, wenn sie „unpopuläre" Maßnahmen wie den Abbau von Parkplätzen oder die Umverteilung von Straßenraum zugunsten des Umweltverbundes beschließen?

Warum wird das Fahrradfahren trotz aller Vorteile in den meisten Städten Europas immer noch diskriminiert? Warum wird die umweltschädlichste und für die Gesamtgesellschaft problematischste Form des urbanen Transports, das Autofahren, weiterhin wider besseres Wissen privilegiert? Warum ist das Thema Fahrradfahren in vielen Ländern Europas so negativ besetzt, warum ist die Opposition so stark, sei sie in den Reihen der Jugendlichen, sei sie bei den Erwachsenen?

14   Vgl. Gill: Children 2005, S. 31ff

Seeking Solutions

Our Project as a Lab

Beauty and the Bike began as an enquiry into why British teenage girls stop cycling. But it soon developed into a project that sought ways of making cycling attractive to girls. We knew from our research that cycling is positively attractive in cycling-friendly cities. So why not learn the lessons from teenage girls from one such city?

First we found the city. Bremen has a strong cycling culture, and the majority of its teenagers use a bicycle every day. Then we found the girls. Obervieland School, a typical secondary school complex in the south of the city with a mix of middle and working class students, had two sociology teachers interested in the social implications of our work. They actively engaged with us around the issues, and from two of their classes we found a group of teenage girls between 16 and 18

Wir suchen eine Lösung

Unser Projekt als Versuchslabor

„Beauty and the Bike" begann als Untersuchung der Frage, warum junge Mädchen in Großbritannien mit dem Fahrradfahren aufhören. Aber dann wollten wir herausfinden, unter welchen Bedingungen die Mädchen Fahrrad fahren würden. Wir wussten, dass es in fahrradfreundlichen Städten hoch attraktiv ist. Warum sollten wir die Mädchen aus den beiden Fahrradkulturen nicht zusammen bringen, damit sie aus erster Hand lernen könnten?

Als erstes haben wir uns dafür entschieden, in Bremen zu arbeiten. Denn Bremen hat eine ausgeprägte Fahrradkultur, und die Mehrheit der Jugendlichen fährt täglich mit dem Rad. Dort fanden wir Mädchen aus dem Gymnasium Obervieland, gelegen im Süden von Bremen in einem Viertel, das eine interessante Mischung aus Arbeiterhaushalten und Mittelschichtfamilien bietet. Zwei

years old. Then we found the bikes. All the girls made it clear to us what they found stylish and attractive (as did most of the boys in their class) – old fashioned dutch bikes. Looking into the bike shop windows in Darlington, we realised that they did not supply the bikes we wanted. So we raised some funds, set up a bike hire scheme and imported them instead.

Our girls in Darlington were fascinated, and started using these bikes immediately: 10 red and black Dutch bikes with hub dynamos, hub gears, back pedal brakes, baskets on the back to carry luggage, skirt guards and strong locks. No girl had to change her fashion, she could use her normal clothes to ride these bikes, so they began to cycle every day.

Enlightenment Leads to Wishes: We Need Cycle Paths!

When the Bremen girls came to Darlington they were taken aback by the conditions offered to cyclists. "To me as a cyclist it was a shock. I did not expect it to be like that, that you are treated like thin air by the cars, that they do not respect you at all and that you have to keep both eyes peeled and to cycle very carefully and dominantly," said one of them. Another simply said that you cannot cycle normally in Darlington. They were shocked by the lack of cycling infrastructure, by the funny looks they got, and by the reckless behaviour of car drivers. They felt like a hunted species, the way drivers were regularly harassing them. The Germans have thoroughly revised their image of the polite Briton.

The girls from Darlington discovered a totally different world for cyclists in Bremen. Car drivers gave them priority, let them have their right of way, they cycled on cycle paths or quiet side roads, and they got wherever they wanted on their bikes. They realised how important cycle paths are if you want to cycle without stress or fear. They actually enjoyed all the many cycle paths, the security to simply start cycling whenever they wanted, knowing they would get anywhere without having to cycle on main roads, yet get there directly and quickly. These experiences, and the feeling of alienation on their return home, lead to their call for cycle paths on main roads in Darlington. Most, though not all, have carried on cycling anyway, the positives outweighing the negatives. But in the

LehrerInnen der Leistungskurse Soziologie waren bereit uns zu helfen, sie interessierten sich für die sozio-politischen Hintergründe unseres Projektes. Aus ihren Kursen der 12. Und 13. Klasse kommen die Mädchen der Bremer Kerngruppe. Und schließlich fanden wir die passenden Fahrräder. Wir wussten mittlerweile, dass Hollandräder total „in" sind. In Darlington konnten wir sie aber in keinem Laden finden, deswegen importierten wir die Räder selbst und entwickelten einen Mini-Fahrrad-Verleih in Darlington.

Unsere Mädchen in Darlington waren begeistert und haben die Räder sofort in Gebrauch genommen: 10 Hollandräder – fast alle rot - mit modernisierter Ausstattung wie einem Nabendynamo, Nabengangschaltung, Rücktrittbremse, Rockschutz, Bügelschloss und einem Fahrradkorb auf dem Gepäckträger.

Erkenntnis führt zu Forderung: Radwege her!

Als die Bremer Mädchen nach Darlington kamen, waren sie von den Bedingungen, die eine RadfahrerIn in Darlington ertragen muss, schlicht entsetzt. „Als Fahrradfahrerin ist das für mich wie so ein Schock gewesen. Ich hab' mir das echt nicht so schlimm vorgestellt, dass man wirklich wie Luft behandelt wird, keine Rücksicht auf uns genommen wird, und dass man schon beide Augen auf halten muss und sehr vorsichtig und sehr dominant durch die Straßen fahren sollte." So kommentierte die Eine. Eine Andere meinte, hier könne sie nicht normal Fahrrad fahren.

Sie waren erschrocken über die mangelnde Fahrrad-Infrastruktur, erstaunt über die entgeisterten Blicke vieler BürgerInnen und entsetzt vom rücksichtslosen Verhalten der meisten AutofahrerInnen und fühlten sich wie Freiwild durch die regelmäßige „Anmache". Sie haben ihr Bild von den höflichen BritInnen gründlich revidiert. Britische AutofahrerInnen sind bei den Bremer Mädchen „unten durch".

Die Mädchen aus Darlington hingegen erlebten eine ganz neue Fahrradwelt in Bremen: AutofahrerInnen ließen ihnen ihre Vorfahrt, sie fanden überall Radwege und kamen mit ihren Rädern überall hin. Sie entdeckten, dass Infrastruktur für Fahrräder das Radfahren einfacher und stressfreier macht. Sie genossen die Sicherheit, dass sie einfach losfahren können, wo immer sie hin wollen, und sich darauf verlassen können, an gefährlichen Straßen Radwege vorzufinden und nicht erschreckt auf Nebenstraßen abbiegen, Umwege in Kauf nehmen zu müssen, um an ihr Ziel zu kommen. Und die Erkenntnis, dass eine gute Fahrradinfrastruktur sich durch Radwege an Straßen auszeichnet, auf denen schnell gefahren wird, hat bei allen Mädchen zu einer simplen und klaren Forderung an die Politik geführt: Sie wollen Radwege an allen Hauptverkehrsstraßen in Darlington.

Die meisten von ihnen fahren auch heute noch Fahrrad, die positiven Seiten überwiegen für sie, aber in Zukunft möchten sie in Darlington ohne Zeitverlust mit ihrem Rad ans gewünschte Ziel kommen, und sie möchten von AutofahrerInnen in Ruhe gelassen werden. Stadträder sind relativ

future they want to cycle in Darlington without losing time or enduring stress from motorists. City bikes are slow in comparison to racing bikes; on the road their slow pace can irritate car drivers. But with cycle paths these bikes would neither irritate cars nor annoy pedestrians.

People of Darlington Want a Change in Transport Policy

Darlington's solid collection of data about travel habits in the town was mentioned earlier. In its second survey in 2008, Socialdata found that 79% of respondents thought it effective if the council further developed bicycle routes and facilities, whilst 59 % want to see car traffic to be limited. But really sensational was this: "For all modes a clear majority of 86% or more of respondents favoured improvements for sustainable travel modes in 2008, even it these disadvantaged car users." [17]
Socialdata also found a huge and growing potential for behaviour change, for reduction in car use: 59 % of local car trips in 2008 were made solely for subjective reasons, without constraints and with at least one sustainable travel mode alternative available. In 2004 this figure lay at 56 %. Moreover 62 % of all car trips were shorter than 5km, a distance that can easily be covered on a bike. [18]

Safe Space for the Bike on Roads:
Hessle Road in Hull and Hamburger Straße in Bremen

Conditions for a change in transport policy in Darlington are ideal. There is a high potential for behaviour change and an overwhelming majority of people would favour improvements for sustainable travel modes even if this disadvantaged car users. "Just a little bit of paint, that's all we need," said one of our girls. She studied the road in Darlington, which she would like to use for her daily trip to work. Woodland Road is wide and inviting, but only for cars. There is no separate cycle path, no space on the pavement, no lane on the road for a bike. But motorists share nearly 12 meters of space even at the narrowest part. A 1.50 meter cycle lane could be painted on each side of the road.
This is exactly what she saw in Bremen, on Hamburger Straße. Here tram, lorries, cars and bicycles once shared a width of 10.25 meter, less than the space on Woodland Road. There are many more

17   Socialdata: Darlington 2009, p. 38
18   See Socialdata: Darlington 2009, p. 42 and table 26

langsam im Verhältnis zu Rennrädern, und auf der Straße kann dieses langsame Dahingleiten AutofahrerInnen irritieren. Aber mit Radwegen an oder neben der Straße wäre sicher gestellt, dass weder Autos noch FußgängerInnen vom Rad gestört würden.

Menschen wollen eine menschenfreundliche Verkehrspolitik

Mit ihren Wünschen stehen unsere Projektmädchen nicht alleine: Dank der umfassenden Erhebungen des Münchner Instituts Socialdata in Darlington ist seit dem März 2005 bekannt, was die BürgerInnen wünschen. Nach der neuesten Befragung aus dem Jahre 2008 halten es 79 Prozent der Befragten für effektiv, die Fahrradinfrastruktur weiter zu entwickeln. Und 59 Prozent möchten dem Autoverkehr Grenzen gesetzt sehen. Doch sensationell ist: Mehr als 86 Prozent wünschen, dass der Umweltverbund gestärkt wird, auch wenn dies den motorisierten Verkehr benachteiligt.[15]

Socialdata hat aber nicht nur eine hohe Bereitschaft der BürgerInnen vorgefunden, den Umweltverbund zu stärken, die Untersuchung der Wege der AutofahrerInnen zeigt darüber hinaus ein hohes Potenzial zum Umstieg: 59 Prozent aller Wege, die mit dem Auto im Jahre 2008 zurück gelegt wurden, hätten durch eine andere Verkehrsmittelwahl ersetzt werden können, denn in 59 Prozent der Wege wurde das Auto nur aus subjektiven Erwägungen gewählt. Es kommt hinzu, dass 62 Prozent aller Autofahrten in 2008 kürzer waren als 5 Km, eine Strecke, die sich mit dem Fahrrad leicht bewältigen lässt.[16]

Sicherer Platz für das Rad auf der Straße: Hessle Road in Hull oder Hamburger Straße in Bremen

Die Voraussetzungen zur verkehrspolitischen Wende in Darlington sind also hervorragend: Es gibt ein hohes Potenzial zum Umstieg vom Auto zum Umweltverbund, und die BürgerInnen würden eine Verschiebung der Privilegien zwischen den Verkehrsgruppen hin zum Umweltverbund mit überwältigender Mehrheit begrüßen.

Mit gutem Willen gäbe es einfache Lösungen: „Just a little bit of paint, that's all we need," sagt eines unserer Mädchen in Darlington. Sie hat sich die Straße in Darlington angeguckt, die sie auf ihrem Weg zur Arbeit nutzen möchte: Woodland Road ist zwar breit und einladend, aber nur für Autos. Es gibt keinen abgeteilten Radweg, keinen Platz auf dem Fußweg und keine Spur

15 86 Prozent im Falle der Förderung des Radverkehrs, 87 Prozent beim ÖPNV und 93 Prozent, wenn die Bedingungen für FußgängerInnen verbessert werden, vgl. Socialdata: Darlington 2009, S. 38
16 Vgl. Socialdata: Darlington 2009, S. 42 und Tabelle 26

fürs Fahrrad. Für den motorisierten Verkehr dagegen sind fast 12 Meter Breite vorgesehen. Hier könnte eine Fahrradspur (1,50 Meter) auf jeder Seite aufgemalt werden.

Genau das hat unsere junge Frau in Bremen in der Hamburger Straße gesehen. Früher teilten sich hier Straßenbahn, LKWs, Autos und Fahrräder einen Straßenraum von 10,25 Metern, das ist weniger Platz als auf Woodland Road. Dazu parkten viele Autos in der zweiten Reihe. Eine unordentliche Straße, a messy road, wird so etwas genannt. Deswegen wurde der Raum für den motorisierten Verkehr auf die Mindestbreite von 6,05 Metern reduziert. Die RadfahrerInnen haben auf beiden Seiten einen Sonderfahrstreifen von jeweils 1,50 Meter erhalten.[17]

Ein solches Modell existiert auch in England. Hull hat auf insgesamt sieben Straßen den Platz neu verteilt, mehr Platz fürs Rad, weniger fürs Auto, und das Ganze mit „just a little bit of paint" und teilweise radikaler als in Bremen. Auf der Hessle Road, die eine vierspurige Straße war, wurden auf 6,2 Kilometer Länge die Außenspuren umgewidmet und zwar zu einem Radweg und stellenweise Parkbuchten. Und es war billig: Pro Meter haben die Huller nur 6 Pfund und 20 Pennies ausgegeben, für insgesamt 24 Kilometer Straßenumbau haben sie 148.303 Pfund Sterling auf den Tisch gelegt. In einer Studie werden die Kosten-Nutzen-Effekte von insgesamt fünf Infrastrukturprojekten zur Förderung des Fahrradverkehrs in England verglichen. Hull hat dabei am besten abgeschnitten.[18] Nur in Hull hat es die Stadtverwaltung gewagt, bestehende Straßen umzuwandeln, dem Autoverkehr Platz zu nehmen und den Straßenraum umzuverteilen. Und auch in London werden jetzt die gleichen Ideen verfolgt.

In Darlington – wie auch in vielen anderen europäischen Kommunen - könnte es viele Hessle Roads und Hamburger Straßen geben, denn hier gibt es viele überbreite Straßen, die auch noch die wichtigsten Arterien in das Stadtzentrum sind, also die schnellste Verbindung von außen nach innen darstellen. Da sie viel Platz bieten, wird schnell gefahren, für FahrradfahrerInnen auf der Straße ein enormer Stressfaktor. Der Stress könnte allen Beteiligten erspart werden, wenn es vernünftige Fahrradwege an viel und schnell befahrenen Straßen gäbe oder eine abgeteilte Fahrradspur auf der Straße. Aber die Radspuren müssen breit genug sein, damit sich FahrradfahrerInnen nicht von den Autos bedrängt fühlen.[19]

Darlington könnte Woodland Road zum Pilotprojekt erklären, die Stadt müsste nicht mehr als 10.000 Pfund für das Anmalen ausgeben, verglichen mit den Kosten von Hull. Bei schmaleren Fahrspuren fahren Autos automatisch langsamer. Langsamer fahrende Autos erzeugen weniger Lärm, weniger CO_2 und weniger Unfälle. Im Gegenzug steigt die Lebensqualität. Was wollen die Darlingtonians mehr?

---

17 Vgl. Zur Hamburger Straße in Bremen: http://www.nationaler-radverkehrsplan.de/praxisbeispiele/anzeige.phtml?id=2054

18 Vgl. SQW Consulting: Planning for Cycling. Report to Cycling England, 18.12.08, www.sqw.co.uk

19 1,50 Meter wäre die Mindestbreite. Vgl. die Times vom 10. September 2009 und Ciaran Meyers/John Parkin: The effect of cycle lanes on the proximity between motor traffic and cycle traffic, Bolton/Leeds 2009. Seit dem 11. August 2009 erhältlich. Vgl. Die Pressemitteilung des CTC vom 10.9.2009: Motorists drive closer to cyclists on cycle lanes: http://www.ctc.org.uk/DesktopModules/Articles/ArticlesView.aspx...

parking spaces on Hamburger Straße than on Woodland Road. The space for motorised traffic on Hamburger Straße was reduced to 6.05 meter, and cyclists got their separate cycle lanes of 1.50 meter each on both sides. [19]

A model like this also exists in Britain. Hull changed 7 of its roads, redistributed the space, more space for bikes, less for motorists, with just "a little bit of paint" - and more radical than in Bremen. Hessle Road, which was a dual-carriage way, was converted into a single lane road, and the kerb-side lanes were handed over to bicycles and parked cars. Per meter Hull invested £6.20, total investment cost for 24 km road: £148,303. In a study, SQW Consulting compared the economic benefit to cost ratio of five cycling projects in England. Hull produced the best ratio of all five, combining low costs with a high rise in the numbers of cyclists.[20] Hull was the only project that dared to retrofit cycling facilities into the existing infrastructure, taking space away from cars and redistributing it to bicycles. London is now waking up to the same idea.

In Darlington (and many other European towns) there could be many Hessle Roads and Hamburger Straßen. There are many over-wide streets, which are also the arterial roads into the town centre, the quickest connection from the rim to the middle. Offering a lot of space, cars speed up and give enormous stress to the few cyclists on these roads. This stress could be relieved, if there were good cycle lanes on fast and busy roads or cycle paths beside them. It would also get more cyclists out on these roads thus reducing congestion. But cycle lanes on the road must be wide enough, if cyclists are not to feel hassled by motor traffic. [21]

The girls in our project could get their wish for a proper, safe cycle path on Woodland Road for less than £10,000, when compared to the cost of the Hull project. Moreover, narrower lanes will slow motor traffic, meaning less noise, less CO_2 and fewer accidents. The quality of life improves for everyone.

Cycle Paths and Real Risk Assessment

When the girls visited Bremen, they also met the politician responsible for transport. His policy is very clear and simple: "On busy roads in the city, we have to separate cyclists and motorists. Anything else is too dangerous." And even in Berlin – which is still not a bicycle city – traffic experts are clear about it: If you have more than 10,000 cars per day on a road with a speed limit of 50 km/h or more, that situation calls for cycle paths. On more than half of its fast and busy

---

19   About Hamburger Straße in Bremen see: http://www.nationaler-radverkehrsplan.de/praxisbeispiele/anzeige.phtml?id=2054

20   See SQW Consulting: Planning for Cycling. Report to Cycling England, 18.12. 2008, www.sqw.co.uk

21   The minimum width should be 1.50 meter. See The Times, 10.9.2009 and Ciaran Meyers/John Parkin: The effect of cycle lanes on the proximity between motor traffic and cycle traffic, Bolton/Leeds 2009. Also press release of CTC, 10.9.09: motorists drive closer to cyclists on cycle lanes: http://www.ctc.org.uk/DesktopModules/Articles/ArticlesView.aspx...

Politik lehnt Radwege ab,
keine verkehrspolitische Wende in Sicht

Als die Mädchen aus Darlington Bremen besuchten, haben sie auch den für Verkehrspolitik verantwortlichen Politiker kennengelernt. Seine Meinung zum Thema Hauptverkehrsstraßen ist klar: „An viel befahrenen Straßen müssen wir Radverkehr und motorisierten Verkehr trennen, alles andere ist zu gefährlich." Auch in Berlin sind sich die ExpertInnen einig: An Straßen mit einer Höchstgeschwindigkeit von 50 km/h und einem Verkehrsaufkommen von 10.000 Autos pro Tag müssen Radwege her, die Hälfte der notwendigen Wege (750 von 1450 Kilometer) hat Berlin bereits abgedeckt.[20]
Andere Politiker sagen es, unsere Mädchen fordern es, die Mehrheit der Bevölkerung von Darlington will es: Nehmt dem motorisierten Verkehr Platz und macht die Straße sicherer für das Rad. Aber die Politik in Darlington, wie auch die meisten britischen PolitikerInnen sagen „nein" dazu. Selbst das Verkehrsministerium in London arbeitet nur mit Empfehlungen, nimmt die Chance nicht wahr, kraft zentraler Autorität Regeln festzulegen, die den schwächeren VerkehrsteilnehmerInnen helfen könnten.[21]
Offenbar will die britische Politik, und da steht sie in Europa nicht alleine, den Konflikt mit dem gehätschelten Autoverkehr nicht aufnehmen. Kritische BeobachterInnen sprechen sogar von einer „Car-Owning Democracy", die „alive und well" ist.[22] „The real barrier is the lack of political will (...) the great majority of authorities see cycling as a bolt-on extra to existing transport policies and are in no way ready to countenance the notion of restraining car traffic in order to make more space for cyclists."[23]
Die Ergebnisse von Socialdata zeigen eindeutig, dass die Menschen in Darlington eine andere Verkehrspolitik wollen. Die Weigerung der Politik zur verkehrspolitischen Wende, diese einseitige Rücksichtnahme auf die autobereifte Wählerschaft dagegen zeugt von ihrer Verlogenheit: Nach außen hin wird gebetsmühlenartig von Gesundheit, Sicherheit und Risikoabschätzung gesprochen. Wenn es aber um wirkliche Gefahrenabwehr, wenn es um die Hauptgefahr auf der Straße geht und es diese zu bannen gilt, dann werden die Töne ganz anders: Bei der Gefahrenquelle Auto wird nicht das Auto entschärft sondern die Gefährdeten haben dafür zu sorgen, dass sie mit dieser Gefahr leben können. Sie müssen als FußgängerInnen auf den Fußweg zurück springen, damit das Auto ungehindert weiter fahren kann, sie müssen als RadfahrerInnen Helme aufsetzen und signalfarbene Kleidung tragen, und sie haben gefälligst an Einmündungen abzusteigen, damit

20 Vgl. Pucher, John/Buehler, Ralph: At the Frontiers of Cycling: Policy Innovations in the Netherlands, Denmark and Germany, in: Whitelegg, John (Hrsg.): World Transport Policy & Practice, Volume 13, Number 3, York 2007, S. 40 und http://www.stadtentwicklung.berlin.de/verkehr/radverkehrsanlagen/de/radwege2.shtml

21 Vgl. Department for Transport. Local Transport Note 2/08, Cycle Infrastructure Design, London October 2008, vgl. Hier z.B. die Ausführungen zu den Radwegen auf der Straße ab Seite 35

22 Vgl. Iain Docherty, Policy, Politics and Sustainable Transport, in: Docherty, Iain/Shaw, Jon (Hrsg.): A New Ideal for Transport? The UK's struggle with the sustainable transport agenda, Malden, Oxford, Carlton 2003, S. 24

23 Tolley, Rodney: Ubiquitous, Everyday Walking and Cycling: The Acid Test of a Sustainable Transport Policy, in: Doherty/Shaw: Transport 2003, S. 192 und Sloman, Lynn: Car Sick. Solutions for our Car-addicted culture, Totnes, Devon 2006, p. 146ff

roads, 750 km of 1450, Berlin has done just that. [22]

So politicians elsewhere say it, the girls in our project say it, the majority of the citizens of Darlington say it – take space from motorised traffic to make it safer for cyclists. But so far, Darlington's local councillors, and indeed most politicians in the UK, say "No". Even the Department for Transport in London only makes recommendations, rather than offering political leadership with this issue. [23] It seems that the UK does not want to tackle motorised traffic – and with this position it is not alone in Europe. Critics call this "Car-Owning Democracy", which is "alive and well". [24] "The real barrier is the lack of political will (...) the great majority of authorities see cycling as a bolt-on extra to existing transport policies and are in no way ready to countenance the notion of restraining car traffic in order to make more space for cyclists." [25]

This refusal to change British transport policy is especially strange looking at the results of Socialdata and people's articulated wishes. The people of Darlington want another transport policy. But it also shows that this society is dishonest. Politicians stress repeatedly the importance of health and safety and risk assessment. But if reality hits in, if the real danger on our roads is identified, the sound of music changes profoundly. Not the source of danger, not the car should be tamed. Instead vulnerable road users have to sort their danger out themselves. As pedestrians they have to jump back on the kerb at junctions, so that his majesty the car can get on with its trip, cyclists should wear security garments like helmets and illuminated vests, and at junctions they should give way, so the car is not stopped.

And even the protecting parents behave in a very contradictory way – not only in the UK: If parents are asked to choose between parking spaces in front of their door, or a road where cars are banned, they do not take their children's safety into account, but choose to be able to park outside their house. [26]

22   See Pucher, John/Buehler, Ralph: At the Frontiers of Cycling: Policy Innovations in the Netherlands, Denmark and Germany, in: Whitelegg, John (Ed.): World Transport Policy and Practice, Volume 13, No. 3, York 2007 and http://www.stadtentwicklung.berlin.de/verkehr/radverkehrs-anlagen/de/radwege2.shtml

23   See Department for Transport. Local Transport Note 2/08, Cycle Infrastructure Design, London October 2008, e.g. p. 35ff about the design of cycle lanes

24   See Docherty, Iain: Policy, Politics and Sustainable Transport, in: Docherty, Iain/Shaw, Jon (Hrsg.): A New Ideal for Transport? The UK's struggle with the sustainable transport agenda, Malden, Oxford, Carlton 2003, S. 24

25   Tolley, Rodney: Ubiquitous, Everyday Walking and Cycling: The Acid Test of a Sustainable Transport Policy, in: Docherty/Shaw: Transport 2003, p. 192, see also Sloman, Lynn: Car Sick. Solutions for our Car-addicted culture, Totnes, Devon 2006, p. 146ff

26   See Knoflacher: Auto 2007

das Kraftfahrzeug ungehindert in den Kreuzungsbereich einfahren kann.

Genauso widersprüchlich verhalten sich die fürsorglichen Eltern – nicht nur in Großbritannien: „Studien belegen übrigens, dass Eltern keine Rücksicht auf ihre eigenen Kinder nehmen, wenn sie zwischen einem Parkplatz vor der Haustür und einer verkehrsberuhigten Zone (in ihrer Wohnstraße, B.W.) wählen müssen. Die Bewegungseinschränkung, ja sogar die Todesgefahr für den eigenen Nachwuchs wird bewusst in Kauf genommen, wenn es um einen möglichst nahe gelegenen Parkplatz geht."[24]

24   Knoflacher: Auto 2007

When will the Bicycle Shop be the Teenager's Paradise all over Europe?

The story of our young women is not over. It is the story of young women all over Europe who want to live free, independent lives, in a world that will have to address the challenges of climate change and the physical well-being of its citizens. The transport challenge for us all is to find ways that make sustainable forms of transport more attractive than less sustainable ones. Yet as the girls in our project have found, we have actual examples of this already in our midst. We only need to listen and learn.

Hints of what is really needed are already in place. Many transport professionals now talk about the hierarchy of transport modes, putting pedestrians and cyclists at the top, and private motorised transport at the bottom of priorities. But this vision needs to be reflected in actual everyday practice. If the car continues to be treated as a first class mode of urban travel, and the bicycle as second class, this hierarchy will only be so much hot air. One practical example of this is to view

Wann kommt das Mädchenparadies Fahrradladen nach ganz Europa?

Die Geschichte unserer Mädchen ist genauso wenig zu Ende wie die aller Frauen in Europa, die unabhängig und frei leben wollen, die sich eine Welt mit weniger Klimawandel wünschen und mehr Lebensqualität. Die Herausforderung im Sinne einer nachhaltigen Verkehrspolitik ist, den Umweltverbund deutlich attraktiver zu machen als den motorisierten Individualverkehr. Unsere Mädchen aus Darlington haben herausgefunden, dass es dafür Beispiele gibt.

Es gibt Zeichen für den Wandel. Viele VerkehrsexpertInnen diskutieren die Hierarchie der Verkehrsmittel neu, ihnen ist klar, dass das Auto gemeinsam mit dem LKW den untersten Platz einnehmen muss, nicht nur auf dem Papier sondern auch in der politisch-legislativen und verwaltungs-exekutiven Realität. FußgängerInnen und RadfahrerInnen gehören ganz nach oben. Diese Erkenntnis muss sich allerdings in den alltäglichen verkehrspolitischen Entscheidungen wiederfinden, denn solange das Auto erster Klasse fährt und das Fahrrad als ein Verkehrsmittel zweiter Klasse behandelt

infrastructure requirements from the point of view of the pedestrian and the cyclist, not the motorist. So where roads are busy, we need cycle paths.

An often used argument is that of the critical mass of cyclists, which would force car drivers to change their behaviour. Once we have enough bicycles on the road, we won't need cycle lanes or paths that separate motorised and non-motorised road users. This view, even proposed by some British cycling campaigns, reflects an extremely male point of view. The on-road cyclist that relishes fighting with cars is typically male. Most women, on the other hand, do not want to have a battle with cars. They want to cycle gently and peacefully, and for that they need their own safe space on main roads. There are plenty of men who would also agree.

This idea that young citizens should fight with middle-aged car drivers whilst elderly politicians sit in peace in their town halls is a sad indictment of the state of mainstream political thinking in the UK. The future of cycling for young women in Britain requires collective measures, by governments and local authorities. Even the humble citizen parent in Darlington, with their feeling of privatised powerlessness, knows that only society as a collective whole can provide the solutions – and is willing to support them. It is the job of politicians to provide the leadership and policy coherence that will deliver these solutions.

If the bicycle is not given open privileges over cars, if the law continues to bow to the maxim "might is right", we shall not see many girls and women cycling in the future, be it in Britain or all over Europe. Then Bremen, Münster and maybe Berlin, Odense and Copenhagen, Groningen and Amsterdam will remain examples of a cycling friendly transport policy.

wird, ist jede Hierarchie nicht besser als das Papier, auf dem sie veröffentlicht wird. Eine praktische Umsetzungsmöglichkeit ist die Neubetrachtung von Hauptverkehrsstraßen aus der Perspektive der RadfahrerIn und nicht durch die Windschutzscheibe. Die Antwort lautet: An Hauptverkehrsstraßen brauchen wir Radwege.

Gerne wird in Großbritannien damit argumentiert, dass das Verhalten der AutofahrerInnen sich automatisch ändern würde, wenn es mehr Fahrräder auf den Straßen gäbe, wenn einfach mehr Menschen vom Auto aufs Fahrrad umstiegen. Das Konzept der notwendigen kritischen Masse ist sehr beliebt, der Masse, die die AutolenkerInnen zur Rücksicht zwänge. Bei vielen Fahrrädern seien dann auch keine Radwege notwendig. Selbst einige britische Fahrradkampagnen unterstützen dieses Argument, wenden sich sogar gegen Fahrradwege an Hauptverkehrsstraßen.

Nach den Erfahrungen mit unserem Projekt können wir nur sagen: Das ist eine bequeme Haltung und zeugt von einer ausgesprochen männlichen Sichtweise. Der so genannte „On-Road Cyclist", dessen Spezies es auch woanders in Europa gibt, kämpft offensichtlich gerne mit dem Auto von Stoßstange zu Schutzblech, in der Mehrheit sind das Männer. Aber dabei fallen die Bedürfnisse der meisten Frauen völlig unter den Tisch: Sie wollen nicht mit Autos auf Straßen kämpfen, sie wollen in Frieden und genussvoll Fahrrad fahren und dafür brauchen sie ihren eigenen, vom Auto abgetrennten Platz auf Hauptverkehrsstraßen. Viele Männer sehen das übrigens auch so.

Was ist das für eine Politik, was für eine Gesellschaft, die von jungen Menschen erwartet, dass sie Konflikte auf den Straßen und mit den Autos austragen, die die Herrschaften im Rathaus nicht wagen anzugehen? Mädchen und Frauen, die in Fahrrad-unfreundlichen Ländern wie Großbritannien Fahrrad fahren wollen, brauchen die aktive Unterstützung der Politik und Administration. Auch die Eltern als Einzelpersonen können nicht alleine die verkehrspolitischen Sünden der vergangenen 40 Jahre beheben. Wenn sie das Vertrauen in die Sicherheit des öffentlichen Raumes für ihre Kinder wieder erlangen sollen, muss die Gesellschaft als Ganzes reagieren, es muss neue Lösungen geben, die Gesellschaft muss sie unterstützen. Und die Politik muss den deutlichen Willen zeigen, dass sie diese Lösungen auch umsetzen wird.

Denn wenn das Fahrrad nicht offensiv bevorteilt wird, wenn nicht die überbordenden Privilegien des Autoverkehrs abgebaut werden, wenn nicht der rechtsfreie Aktionsraum des Autos wieder rechtsstaatlichen Prinzipien unterworfen wird, wird es auch in Zukunft wenige Mädchen und Frauen in ganz Europa geben, die gerne und alltäglich Fahrrad fahren. Dann werden auch in Zukunft Bremen und Münster (Berlin?), Odense und Kopenhagen, Groningen und Amsterdam (neben anderen hier nicht erwähnten Orten) klimafreundliche Inseln im europäischen Fahrrad-feindlichen Verkehrsmeer bleiben.

This project has just given birth to a baby daughter called DarLOVElo. She is going to work with local bicycle shops to make attractive, stylish Dutch and other city bikes much more widely available to the people of Darlington. The bicycle trade, through its organisation Bike Hub, is supporting the girls from Beauty and the Bike to run a Bike Pool of around 100 dutch bikes. If successful, this will become the model for similar projects up and down the country. Once these bicycles appear in the shop windows in Darlington and perhaps one day all over Britain, then I can start dreaming my childhood dream of the bicycle shop with pleasure. But most of all I wish that all Europe's young people can live my dream, in a world with less cars, more bikes, more freedom and independence, less climate change and loads of heavenly bicycle shops. As one of our girls said, "We've got the lovely girls, we've got the lovely bikes. Now all we need are the lovely cycle paths".

Eine Tochter von „Beauty and the Bike" ist DarLOVElo, unser Low-Cost-Fahrradverleih. DarLOVElo wird mit lokalen Fahrradläden zusammen arbeiten, um schicke Hollandräder und praktische City Bikes für möglichst viele Menschen in Darlington erreichbar zu machen. Der Fahrradhandel, in persona seine Organisation „Bike Hub", wird den Erwerb und Verleih von rund 100 Stadträdern unterstützen. Wird das Modell ein Erfolg, soll es über ganz Großbritannien verbreitet werden.

Wenn solche Räder überall in den Schaufenstern stehen, kann ich auch in Darlington und vielleicht bald in ganz Europa mit Genuss meinen Kindertraum vom Fahrradladen leben. Am meisten aber wünsche ich mir, dass alle Kinder und Teenager in ganz Europa meinen Traum träumen können, dass sie aufwachen und eine menschlichere Welt vorfinden, mit weniger Autos, mit mehr Fahrrädern, mehr Freiheit und Unabhängigkeit, mit weniger Klimawandel und ganz vielen traumhaften Fahrradläden. Wie sagte eines der Mädchen in Darlington? „We've got the lovely girls, we've got the lovely bikes. Now all we need are the lovely cycle paths."

Authors

Beatrix Wupperman, born in 1952, is an economist and environmental campaigner.
She is based in Bremen, Germany.
Richard Grassick, born in 1953, is a film-maker and photographer based in Darlington, UK.
He worked with Newcastle-based collective Amber for 23 years before going freelance in 2006.

Producer

Darlington Media Group is a user-run media facility based in Darlington. UK. Founded in 1982, it
supports media production, education and exhibition. www.mediaworkshop.org.uk

Picture Credits

Sabine Bungert | cover, cover rear, pages: 4, 8 right, 9, 10, 11, 20, 24, 38 left, 44, 47, 52 both
top, 56, 59, 60, 61
Phil Dixon | pages: 5, 6, 8 left, 12, 13, 15, 16, 23, 25 both, 28, 29, 32, 33, 34, 38 right, 41, 42,
46, 48, 52 bottom, 62, 63, 64, 66, 67, 68, 69, 70

  Heinrich Böll Stiftung ⊹ Bremen

This project has been funded with support from the European Commission. This publication reflects the views only of the authors, and the Commission
cannot be held responsible for any use which may be made of the information contained therein.